It Works if You Work It

D1069483

Published by
Emotions Anonymous International Services
Post Office Box 4245
Saint Paul, Minnesota 55104-0245
United States of America

ISBN: 0-9607356-9-0

All shall be well, and all shall be well, and all manner of things shall be well.

-14th century, Dame Julian of Norwich

Table of Contents

Letters From the Trustees and the Director

Dear Fellow EA Members,

You may be wondering why we decided that another EA book should be developed at this time. All of us sincerely felt that our fellowship needed a piece of literature that spoke directly about how others live the Twelve Steps. How do we grow in spirituality despite the inevitable ups and downs of working the EA program? What can we share with one another to make our 12-step paths easier?

We know that you will find within this book a connection to all EA members around the world. The sharing and comments offered here emphasize the individual ways in which we each apply the steps to our lives. This information will aid us in recommitting ourselves to the work of the program.

As trustees, it is gratifying for us to assist the EA International Service Center and EA members in any way we can. *It Works if You Work It* is one way to share our collective experiences, strength and hope with others. We believe you will find the book to be a source of inspiration as you seek to live each day through the Twelve-Step program of Emotions Anonymous.

Sincerely, EA Board of Trustees

Dear Readers,

I am so pleased with our new book and grateful that I was able to play a part in its creation.

The first trickle of an idea for this book came from a class that I teach at a local university. My students are assigned the topic of writing their own interpretations of the 12 Steps. I have been very enthusiastic about and impressed with their original thinking on the steps. I began to save many of these papers in hope of someday doing something useful with them (see *Students of the Twelve Steps,* page x).

Then, over a short period of time, several EA members approached me to discuss the very different strategies they employed to work the 12 Steps more effectively. Finally, Mary, the woman who would eventually author this book, contacted me. She inquired about any volunteer or freelance work she could do for the EA program. I started to get the message that there was some kind of action being required of me—this series of events seemed to be more than coincidence.

I presented my thoughts regarding a new book to the Book and Literature Committee in September 2001, and they, in turn, suggested the idea to the Board of Trustees. I received the go-ahead to begin work on the volume and got in touch with Mary, who had done a previous piece on EA called *Like a Shoe That Pinches** (reviewed in *The New Message*, Volume 1, 1999). She and I brainstormed ideas and began to develop an outline for the book. This was presented to the Executive Committee in April 2002, and by September 2002, we had received approval from the entire board.

As I write this, *The New Message* editor, Karen Andersen, and myself are evaluating and editing the first rough draft of the book. Our working draft will be forwarded to a Book and Literature subcommittee for final review.

Being part of this project has been a wonderful experience. EA members have been generous in submitting materials and ideas. Past and present trustees have offered their thoughts and guidance. The author is knowledgeable, precise, and talented and it has been delightful to collaborate with her.

Thank you all for allowing me to play a part in the formation of this very special book.

In EA Service and Fellowship,
Karen Mead
Executive Director

Like a Shoe That Pinches, Carrie Connelly, 1999, Old Mountain Press, Inc.

Author's Introduction

I would like to first thank all EA members and staff who helped contribute to this book. Your generosity of spirit, and the gift of your time in preparing thoughtful responses to our members' survey, was truly inspiring.

Researching and writing *It Works if You Work It* has been a life-altering experience for me. I have grown both personally and professionally, and have changed many of the ways in which I work my EA program.

Before I began the book, I felt that I was at a plateau in my program. Yes, I was going through all the motions, reading the literature, attending meetings, and even offering services ranging from becoming a sponsor to starting a meeting. But I felt that the program was no longer energizing my daily activities or inspiring me to reach deeper.

The techniques and tools I learned in writing this book required me to leave my comfort zone, expand my program, and begin the practices of meditation and self-evaluation which have so richly added to my life. My automatic responses began to change very slowly, and I found myself more willing to let go of the burdens of the past and be at peace in mind and body.

At last I've learned the true meaning of *turning it over*.

Each day as I sat down to write, I would shut my eyes and turn over my thoughts and actions to the care of my Higher Power. The result is a book that truly offers fresh ideas for working the program.

The mission of Emotions Anonymous is to carry a message of hope to people who seek emotional wellness. I believe that this text, coupled with dedication to working the program, will transform that hope into a measure of serenity that we can all carry into our everyday lives.

As we sometimes say at the close of our EA meetings, "Keep coming back. It works if you work it."

Mary, Author
International Service Center

Part I

How Do You
Work It?

PART I—How Do You Work It?

Let me remember how the dawn breaks in the morning.
The change from darkness into light comes on so
gradually it is hardly noticeable.

Twelve Powerful Suggestions

As the Emotions Anonymous program passes the 30-year mark and embraces a new century, it is important to remember that we choose the steps—they don't choose us.

Alcoholics Anonymous literature, including such books as the *Twelve Steps and Twelve Traditions,* frequently mentions that the steps "are just suggestions." They are not commands from our Higher Power, nor are they written in stone.

They are simply guidelines for living in a more emotionally healthy way, with an emphasis on inner peace and serenity. We needn't feel worried that we are not working every step correctly, or even that there is a single correct way to go about it.

1

Having freely chosen to live our lives according to these very important suggestions called the Twelve Steps, we will want to see progress in our ability to apply the principles of the program to our daily lives. We'll stretch ourselves to make some or all of the Twelve Promises come true and bring a message of hope to others.

It's only human, after all, to want to get better at something we work at, to avoid becoming frustrated or giving up. Joining in fellowship with other members is very important, as is a willingness to practice the steps. The tough part is putting in the hard work, patience, and effort needed to travel to the top of these steps.

Most of us join EA because our lives are hard. We are very familiar with the daily struggles involved in working one or two jobs, maintaining our homes or apartments, feeding and caring for ourselves and our families, and keeping our relationships intact.

We come into the program to find release from all that. There is release, serenity, and sane thinking here, and there are many ways to make the efforts necessary to grow in the practice of the EA program. Attending meetings, becoming involved and active in your home group, spending time reading program literature, sharing on the EA Loop internet system, making phone calls, meditating, or praying can be key to making the steps real for us.

This book offers us some new thoughts and tools to help us succeed in working the program and evaluating our progress in EA. These ideas come from members just like you: people who have struggled with working the program and want to share their insights. The power of the program is that many people work toward a single goal: serenity, peace of mind, and the ability to live with unsolved problems.

The chapters in this book present the words and experiences of members around the world who have found that they are more than their emotional problems—they are part of the strength of this fellowship and the goodness of a Higher Power.

Special thanks to Alcoholics Anonymous, from which the EA program and much of the literature has been adapted over the years.

> *Help me to seek the bright light of awareness*
> *and the knowledge of what and where I am.*
>
> -Today, January 29

Where Are We Now, Where Are We Going?

Before we can take a look at the opportunities and

challenges facing Emotions Anonymous in the future, we have to develop a clear picture of who we are.

EA is a vibrant service organization with over 1000 groups in 32 countries around the world. About half of all EA groups are located in the US, with additional concentrations in Germany and Canada. Past surveys have shown that the average EA group has about 10 members, approximately 60 percent of whom are female. The average group member age is late forties.

There are seven EA regions in the US and two in Canada, each of which has a regional trustee. The regional system is complemented by a number of intergroups which help draw the groups together, plan local activities, and order EA literature. EA has 14 intergroups in the US and seven in Canada. The EA Board of Trustees comprises nine regional trustees, three general service trustees, three non-member trustees, and an executive director.

Starting in 1972 as an offshoot of a program called Neurotics Anonymous, EA rented its first office space in 1974 in St. Paul, MN, where the office is headquartered today. The EA International Service Center has a small staff that fills literature and information requests, produces the *The New Message* magazine quarterly, edits and oversees production of new literature, and serves as the coordination point for the annual EA convention. The convention changes locations from year to year and is open to anyone seeking to become well emotionally. EA is funded through book and literature sales and member contributions. It is a non-profit organization with 501(c)3 status. Personal donations to EA are tax-deductible, depending on varying tax laws.

In addition to weekly meetings, groups may band together to offer annual or semi-annual retreats or workshops within their locality. Many intergroups also sponsor a telephone service that can direct callers to the groups nearest them. Each EA group is responsible for holding information meetings, posting flyers, running ads or otherwise letting the public know what EA is all about and where they can go to attend a meeting.

This system of "attraction rather than promotion" is rounded out by the EA website, www.emotionsanonymous.org, where anyone can find out more about the program and access a meeting schedule. The EA Loop (see page 24) is yet another tool that can help draw new members into the program, and is a way for all EA members to share their feelings with others. Loop members also have the opportunity to meet face-to-face at the annual convention, which often features such special activities as a Loopers Breakfast.

Now that we have an understanding of how our

organization works, we can focus on some of the challenges placed before us. First among them is the problem of sustaining a complex global organization with limited funds. This is a problem common to many non-profit groups. Another dilemma involves ensuring that as many people as possible know that EA is available. It's important, also, to help nurture individual groups and encourage the start of new ones. The goal is to see that there are enough groups so that almost everyone can attend a face-to-face meeting near them. Maintaining consistent groups, helping members start new groups, and encouraging all members to become involved in service and donation to their groups is difficult.

These challenges are more than offset by the positive changes EA has seen over the years. Literature has become more diverse and helpful, communication has been enhanced with the advent of the computer and the Internet, and EA members—the true strength of the program—have remained the core of the organization. Members tell us that although they, too, have problems with establishing and continuing groups, they are completely committed to the program. They say the program saved their lives and they want to be there to help others just like them.

This is the spirit that founded EA and that continues to ensure that the program is there for future generations. All any of us can do is share our talents and skills to the best of our ability and leave the outcome and the future in the care of our Higher Power. That is the EA way.

Thank You for these simple, effective tools.

-Today, July 3

What EA Is...and Is Not

EA is such an inclusive group that anyone desiring emotional health is welcome. At times, it seems the group can be all things to all people. However, there are some things that EA *is* and some things it is *not*. Here they are:

- EA *is* led by members. Meeting duties should rotate among all members. Directors, trustees, sponsors, or meeting leaders do *not* have authority over members.
- EA *is* about equality. The spirit of EA is *not* represented by any one person giving directions or guidelines to members of other groups around the country.
- EA's literature *is* important in helping members work the steps. The literature is *not* required reading, but it does carry the central message of our program. Some of us may have the notion that if members purchase and

study EA literature, they will decide to work the program at home rather than attending meetings. Not true; literature usually enhances meeting participation. We believe that putting extra information about the program in the hands of members is always a good thing. The decision to attend face-to-face meetings or not is entirely up to each EA member.

- EA *is* non-confrontational. We do *not* take members aside to suggest immediate actions they must take to become well. We offer quiet assistance and guidance. We inspire others by our example; we do not give advice.

- EA *is* an important part of emotional wellness for many people and can be worked as a member chooses. The EA program need *not* be followed so rigidly that those who aren't sponsored (or those who aren't making obvious progress in their recovery) are looked down upon or discouraged from attending meetings.

- EA *is* open to anyone seeking emotional health, regardless of their race, religion, sexual preference, style of dress, or personality type. However, we do abide by the the concepts and traditions of the program. We can *not* allow members to act in such an overbearing, pushy, sarcastic, mocking, or threatening manner that they scare away newcomers. An EA meeting is a place where all members should feel safe and respected.

- EA *is* a spiritual—*not* a religious—program. Groups are not encouraged to say special prayers (other than the Serenity Prayer) during meetings. People of all faiths, as well as atheists and agnostics, should feel welcome at our meetings and a part of our program. Members may feel free to substitute "Higher Power" or another term for "God" in reading our literature.

- The EA meeting *is* a peaceful, neutral space for groups to gather. It is *not* the place for religious or political discussion, or for the use of non-EA sanctioned material. EA meetings should not be the sales or distribution point for cosmetics, cookies, health aides, non-EA books, chain letters, or the like.

- EA members' experiences *are* theirs alone. They are *not* a standard to be met, or a way of offering direct instruction to other members.

- EA *is* supportive of all positive actions that members take to regain and maintain their mental and emotional health. We *do not* discourage visits to psychiatrists, taking medication, or the like.

- If a group *is* following the above guidelines, as well as the concepts and traditions of EA, it is considered an EA group. If a group does *not* follow these principles, it is simply a gathering of like-minded people. EA does not lend or sell its program name to non-EA groups.

Many of us have never considered the fact that EA has a long and rich history. From this history, program members draw on the wisdom of experience to adapt to the needs of our changing society. Here's a glance at some EA milestones:

EA History in a Timeline

4/12/66   The first Minnesota Neurotics Anonymous group (which would later become one of the first Emotions Anonymous groups) is started with the support of several Al-Anon members.

6/15/71   Minnesota Intergroup Association is incorporated.

7/6/71   Minnesota Intergroup Association votes to disassociate from Neurotics Anonymous.

7/29/71   Written permission is received from the World Service Office of Alcoholics Anonymous to use the 12 Steps and 12 Traditions in conjunction with our program.

8/1/71   The *You Are Not Alone* pamphlet—currently titled *EA's Twelve-Step Program,* and affectionately referred to as the Yellow Pamphlet—is first published.

8/9/71   In Germany, Neurotics Anonymous members vote to disassociate from NA and join EA.

1/1/72   The first issue of *Carrying the EA Message* is published. This monthly publication costs $3 a year.

4/23/72 A decision is made to publish a quarterly International Services Bulletin.

10/14/72 The first annual EA Convention is held in St Paul, Minnesota. The original EA bylaws are ratified by the membership.

6/28/75 Bylaws are amended to allow for non-member trustees.

1976   The German *Intergruppe* is formed. The Intergruppe is still in existence today, serving almost 300 German EA groups.

12/15/76 The first nonmember trustees are appointed to the board.

1978   There are 202 groups in 8 countries.

8/17/78 The original *Emotions Anonymous* book is printed. By October, the first 1,000 copies have sold and more need to be bound.

1979   EA is established in French-speaking Canada, in Montreal. Today there are more than 70 groups in that area.

5/14/82 The German translation of the *Emotions Anonymous* book is presented at their Tenth Anniversary meeting in Hamburg, Germany.

7/9/83   A unity meeting is held in an attempt to resolve issues that have arisen between the board of trustees and the membership.

7/1/87   *Sélection du Reader's Digest*, a French version of the *Reader's Digest*, talks about EA in an article entitled *Apprenez à vivre avec le stress*.

8/1/87   The *Enquirer* runs an article on EA that results in large bags of mail to the International Service Center (ISC).

9/1/87   EA is mentioned as a resource in an article in *Better Homes & Gardens*.

11/21/87 The *Today* meditation book is published.

1988   There are 1,451 EA groups in 28 countries.

1989   The first EA group in France is founded.

12/7/89 EA is mentioned in an *Ann Landers* column, which results in many new members.

10/1/89 EA is mentioned in a *Reader's Digest* article entitled *Let Go and Live.*

9/14/90 The annual EA convention is held in Montreal, Canada. It is the first time that the convention is held outside the United States.

7/1/92   The EA medallion, designed by members, becomes available. The bottom portion is flat, rather than rounded, to symbolize that our recovery is ongoing and never complete.

1994   The Japanese translation of *Today* is received at the ISC.

9/18/94 A major revision to the bylaws (two years in the making) is ratified by the membership at the annual meeting. The revised bylaws move EA from a St. Paul- centered board of trustees to a regional representation system.

1995   Most EA literature is revised by a very hard-working Literature Committee.

4/20/95   The first shipment of the revised *Emotions Anonymous* is received at the ISC. Some 15,000 copies are ordered for the initial printing.

6/21/96   The first EA World Convention is held in Hamburg, Germany. It is attended by more than 600 people from many parts of the world, including Austria, Belgium, England, France, Germany, Liechtenstein, Sweden, Switzerland, and the United States.

1996   Our website first appears on the Internet. Today it can be viewed in English, Japanese, Spanish, or Swedish and provides links to National Intergroups in French-speaking Canada, French-speaking Europe, Germany, and Russia.

1997   The EA Loop is established. Shortly thereafter, the first online meeting takes place.

1998   There are 1,239 groups in 36 countries.

6/15/98   The domain name of *EmotionsAnonymous.org* is registered.

10/1/98   A decision is made to combine *The Message* and the

International Services Bulletin into one quarterly publication called *The New Message.* The publication is provided to groups on a complimentary basis.

2003   Portions of EA materials have now been translated into 20 different languages.

2003   There are just over 1,000 groups in 32 countries. For the past three years, our group count has increased slightly each year.

7/1/03   Projected date for when this book goes to press!

You may be wondering, though, how 12-step programs themselves came into being. We've found a number of highlights throughout the early years of these programs. These are worth mentioning:

Twelve Step Timeline

1908   While traveling in Europe, a YMCA secretary has a spiritual transformation that changes his life. He goes to nearby Oxford University and forms an evangelical group to share his experience.

1908   The movement, now called the Oxford Group, spreads to many other countries, including the USA. The USA group is housed in a church in New York City, and begins to attract new members.

1934   A childhood friend of Bill W (who helped start AA) is about to be jailed for chronic alcoholism. Three men from the Oxford Group visit him; later that year he discusses the principles of the Oxford program with Bill W.

1934   Bill W meets with his friend Dr. Bob in Akron, Ohio, and they begin to think about and share some of the principles of the Oxford Group program. They form the first Alcoholics Anonymous (AA) group.

1938   The Twelve Steps, which come as an inspiration to Bill W., are written for the first time.

1939   The first edition of the AA *Big Book* is published.

1950's   A new group called Al-Anon, specifically for the families of alcoholics, gains in popularity.

      AA begins to give permission for other programs to adopt AA's 12-step principles and guidelines. Each group changes the wording of the steps and guidelines slightly to meet the needs of its members. These groups are collectively referred to as "Anonymous" programs.

Thank you for the differences in people,
which truly spices up the adventures of living.

-Today, October 21

Groups Around the Globe

Where could it ever be easier to unite people of all nationalities, faiths, and life circumstances in a heartfelt search for emotional wellness than in EA?

Emotions Anonymous reaches out to needy human beings everywhere, from those in far-off countries to those who are imprisoned. The EA program is also there for members who have developed their own types of groups to suit their needs.

Here are some of the things these groups had to say:

Okurayama Group in Yokohama, Japan—We meet two times a week at two different places in Yokohama City. One meeting is a step meeting, the other is a general theme meeting. We have 8-12 members, 70 percent of whom are women, and our average age is 35. We speak Japanese.

We think that one of the most important roles in EA is that of sponsor. The sponsor listens to another's troubles, worries, sorrows, anger, and pleasures without preaching. Working our program means to participate in EA independently and to use the 12 Steps every day in our lives.

Sweden—Our group meets every Sunday afternoon. We have only 3-5 regular members, all of whom are men. We sometimes have newcomers who attend a 12-step treatment center in our neighborhood, and most of these are women. We use the regular meeting format for the first part of the meeting. If we have a step meeting, we read the step and then share. At the end of the meeting, I usually read my translation of the *Today* book, then we read the traditions, and finish with the serenity prayer. We speak Swedish.

Working the program, for us, means first making our meetings work. Continuity and fellowship are very important, and with no meeting, it's hard to keep working the program. Many things we have to do on our own, of course: step work, coming to believe, turning the will over to the care of God, writing the inventory and sharing it, becoming ready to have God change us, meditation, and praying.

The EA program applies fairly well to our country and culture, but I don't think that people everywhere accept these ideas. There are people who don't like the "God stuff," then there are people who don't think it's Christian enough and want to talk about Jesus. I also think there is a suspicion that 12-step groups are anti-medication. We need to be clear on this point when we approach people.

I was listening to the radio the other day and heard one person's opinion that 12-step movements caused problems. The guest argued that programs like AA and EA make all problems personal, and cloud the need for change throughout our society. I thought this was interesting.

I want to say to all of you out there, keep going, we are all in this together. We are all important people trying to light a candle of hope in this time in which we are living.

Wuppertal, Germany—We meet weekly, welcome newcomers, read from the *You Are Not Alone* pamphlet, introduce ourselves, and tell something about how each of us is feeling today, or our experiences. Then we choose a topic. Every first Monday of the month is a step meeting and we read from the text. We close with "flashbacks," wherein we tell how we are feeling in the moment or what the meeting has given us. We speak German, have on average

8-16 people, 60 percent women, average age of 40. I sometimes reflect that EA in Germany is growing older—we used to attract more people in their early 20's.

In general, the EA program applies well to our culture. Most of our members suffer from fear, depression, shame, obsessions and compulsions, and some of us use the other parts of the program (the slogans, the pamphlets) more than the steps. I do sometimes ask myself, though, if the EA program applies more to our current generation than to others. Things have changed in our society over the years, and young people nowadays may not be able to understand 12-step programs. Maybe we need to look into literature and outreach more tailored to young people.

Salcete, Goa, India—At our Sunday meetings, we have more than 50 people, while our Thursday meetings attract less than 20. Ours is a joint meeting, with both Al-Anon and EA, so we follow standard AA/EA practices. AA and Al-Anon are very widespread in India. So far we have no EA sponsors, but we do have AA sponsors.

We request prayers from EA members everywhere for the growth and spread of the EA message to more people who are victims of chronic emotional pain.

Canada—We follow the yellow pamphlet for the most part. As far as dealing with group behaviors, we try to address these issues in our weekly meetings. We had one member, for example, who continually violated Concept 12 (confidentiality). We put this concept on our meeting agenda for the next week and that solved the problem.

One unique method we've found for working the Fourth Step is looking at the four basic dimensions of life: Where did we come from? Who are we right now? What gifts have we been given? What are we doing with the gifts we've been given?

Australia—We traditionally meet weekly, with an average of 5-7 members. Our meetings are 60 percent women and our average age is 45 to 50. We have some sponsors, but usually not enough to go around.

The concept of admitting to emotional illness doesn't fit our cultural heritage of the tough, independent, sports-mad Aussie. It's now okay to admit to depression, anxiety, or mental illness, but not to having problems with your emotions. We are seen as weak even when we admit to having emotions, and this is a huge hurdle for us to overcome.

Our customs or language may differ, but we all share the pain as well as the hope of recovery from that pain. Your story may be different from mine, but the pain sure feels just as bad to me as it does to you. Let's continue sharing our stories and our pain, and together we can live just this one day.

Tylers Green, United Kingdom—Our meeting has 6-12 members and is 60 percent women. Some of us have sponsors, some do not. We meet weekly and select a topic for discussion. The topics are either raised by members or drawn from a basket of suggestions that members have written down and submitted anonymously. We discuss each of the steps in turn every fourth week.

As far as the program applying to our culture, there is a general belief that people are more open to sharing about their emotions in the US than in the UK.

One interesting question is this: How does a Christian-based program like EA apply to Muslims, Hindus, Buddhists, and all those with other ideas about and names for God?

[Editor's Note: EA is a spiritual program, not a Christian-based program. Members may use the term Higher Power or another term in place of God.]

Huntsville, Texas, Prison Group—EA has about 27 prison groups in the US, primarily in Texas and Michigan. The two meetings I go to average 8-10 men each, and we do follow the traditional meeting format.

Most of our members have been imprisoned long-term and also attend AA or NA (Narcotics Anonymous). Our members are attracted to EA because of a desire to discuss their feelings rather than their previous substance abuse. EA helps them cope with sadistic employees, cellmates who act out, and the general tedium of life behind bars.

For most of the men, it has been an eye-opener to realize that their addiction problems and the life of crime they were leading were affected by their emotions. Most have surrendered to a Higher Power willingly and use the tools of the program—particularly the *Today* book—to keep them focused one day at a time.

The men really appreciate receiving EA materials donated by other EA members or groups. Anyone interested in helping out in this way, or in helping start a prison group near them, should contact the EA International Service Center.

Burnsville, Minnesota, Study Group—This Twin Cities area group has been meeting twice a month since 2002. Our goal has been to study the steps in a way that is more in-depth than that of a traditional EA meeting.

We also concentrate on the importance of sponsorship,

and on supporting each other in working Steps Four and Five. We believe that the "meat" of each step is contained in only a few paragraphs, which we study for clues about the direct actions we must take to complete that step.

I am not afraid to stumble any more:
Your support brings balance to my life.

-Today, January 5

What Is the Loop?

If you've ever had a best friend or adult child move away, you know the value of that simple note of encouragement, phone call or e-mail. EA has its own system to allow you to share your feelings with a large number of members around the world: the EA Loop. This can be a key tool in helping you move forward in the EA program, particularly if you don't live near a face-to-face meeting or are homebound. Daily shares and the opportunity for online sponsorship make this a cornerstone of the program for many EA members worldwide.

The Loop is a confidential computer internet service provided and regulated by the Emotions Anonymous

International Service Center. Even if you're not a computer expert, joining and using the Loop is easy. Just send an e-mail to info@emotionsanonymous.org asking that the staff add your address to the list of those enrolled. You will receive a welcome note outlining the guidelines for the Loop (see page 28).

The Loop is a way of accessing many EA members with a single writing. Members share the responsibility of posting the daily *Today* readings. Many share their responses to the reading. Other members talk about the sad or joyful times they're experiencing, difficulties with anxiety, depression, panic, or even the daily blessings that we all experience in our everyday lives. When you hit the *Reply* button to respond to a member's share, you send your note directly to that person. Thoughts, feelings or ideas that you'd like to share with the entire group can be addressed to e-anon@mtn.org.

This ingenious computer communication system was developed in 1997 and now has about 150 members in several countries. Only about 20 percent of Loop members share regularly, with some posting daily shares. Others are sustained by just reading the insightful 12-step reflections posted by members. Flawed typing or grammar skills, or even poor familiarity with the English language, don't matter much here. This is a place where you can feel free to express your innermost thoughts without concern about being judged—just like you're attending a regular EA meeting.

Why use the Loop? Well, it relieves the feelings of isolation felt by those who live far from major cities, or who are confined to their homes by illness, old age, or very young children. Those who work on computers or travel frequently find that Loop shares provide a welcome relief from all the work and junk e-mail they wade through each day. Also, a member may post a share that touches a nerve for you in a certain way, as you read it in the silence and comfort of your own home. Other members may offer suggestions for unique ways to work the program, or even offer tips for facing your fourth step, praying, or meditating. If you're new to computers, the Loop can be a place where you feel safe to experiment and learn more.

Loop members tell us the service has been extremely important in making them feel that they are not alone and that they are listened to and respected just as they are, even with all their fears and faults. Here are some thoughts our members shared:

> The Loop is great. Of course, anonymity is at its peak there. I can just talk, just log on, no excuses about getting to the meeting. The Loop is very important to me because it is always there

and it's some kind of contact with real people.

-Yael

I try to stay in touch with the Loop. It is good
to know that there are people all over this globe
 working the program.

-Jakob

I get much comfort from the Loop, although I'm
guilty of not posting a great deal to it. I am
primarily a listener, not a talker.

-Jim

In addition to the EA Loop, some members have organized
an EA online chat room. The chat room address is: http://
groups.yahoo.com/group/emotions-anonymous/chat.   Here
you will be walked through the registration process,
including the process of joining this special EA Chat Room
(different from the EA Loop), and you'll receive a Yahoo ™
ID. Anyone is welcome to share, but you must have a Yahoo™
ID and Yahoo™ e-mail address to access the chat room.

Registration must be approved, so plan on a delay of a day
or two before you can begin participating. Any member can
use the chat room at any time, but there are also regular

meetings held. You will be notified of these electronically once your registration is approved. You can go to the chat room address, http://groups.yahoo.com/group/emotions-anonymous, or address any questions to the following e-mail address: emotions-anonymous-owner@yahoogroup.com

The same behavior guidelines for face-to-face meetings and EA Loop communications apply to online chat room meetings. The cornerstone of these guidelines is the 12 Concepts, which can be found on our website at www.emotionsanonymous.org

Here are the parameters for the use of this technology:

Loop Guidelines

- The Loop is not a place where we judge each other's spelling or grammar. We are all here to share our experience, strength and hope with others.
- We do not use inappropriate or abusive language. Should this occur, the writer would be removed from the Loop.
- We do not discuss religion, religious beliefs or politics, nor do we promote outside issues.
- Personal responses (*I enjoyed your share, here are some ideas . . .*) should be directed to the writer, not to the group. The reply button allows you to reply directly to the writer. To share with the larger group, e-mail your

message to <u>e-anon@mtn.org</u>

• It is important to keep our writing EA related. We do not send poems, jokes, or stories written by others. All writings should be original. We do not send greeting cards, or include the Loop address as part of broadcast messages from other Internet sites.

• What is written on the Loop is confidential. Information should not be repeated or shared without the permission of the writer. If a member makes a personal response to our share that, too, remains confidential.

• At times the Service Center will receive a message regarding a Loop address that reads *permanent fatal address* or *mailbox full*. When this happens, the subscriber is automatically removed from the Loop. If you find you're not receiving your Loop mail, send a note to <u>info@emotionsanonymous.org</u> This is also the address you use if you choose to unsubscribe from the Loop.

• The Loop must be self-supporting. Send your voluntary contributions to EA International, PO Box 4245, St. Paul, MN 55104-0245.

• These Loop guidelines are distributed on the first day of the month to all members.

Part II

Reflections on the Steps

May I keep seeking, as in Step 11,
to improve my conscious contact with You.

-Today, January 14

The 12 Principles and the Beauty of the Steps

In the 1950's, Alcoholics Anonymous groups began informally sharing what has become known as the Principles of the 12 Steps. Each step has a corresponding principle that one can keep in mind when working the step. They are as follows:

Step 1: Honesty

Step 2: Hope

Step 3: Faith

Step 4: Courage

Step 5: Integrity

Step 6: Willingness

Step 7: Humility

Step 8: Responsibility

Step 9: Justice

Step 10: Perseverance

Step 11: Spiritual awareness

Step 12: Service

These principles can best be understood in the context of reflections on each of EA's 12 Steps. For example, Step One is our introduction to the program: *We admitted we were powerless over our emotions—that our lives had become unmanageable.* Just to walk through the door of our first EA meeting requires a level of **honesty** that many of us may never have known before.

We honestly admit to ourselves that we are having trouble functioning and we need help, and then we seek out that help and sit down with strangers in a public space to work on this problem. Maybe we don't participate actively in the meeting at first, and maybe we balk at the words "powerless" and "unmanageable." But we soon realize that on our own we had not been able to solve our problems; willpower and resolve had not changed our negative behaviors and attitudes. We see that our lives had been gradually consumed by anxieties and fears and that we could no longer face the everyday frustrations and challenges that are part of our human existence. This, too, is a new level of self-honesty and our first step up the ladder to serenity.

As we embark on Step Two, *Came to believe that a power greater than ourselves could restore us to sanity,* we begin to be optimistic that the simple act of "coming to believe" offers us **hope** for improved emotional health. If we have been reviewing the literature and reflecting on the steps, when we come into the meeting our eyes are opened to others in the group. We begin to really hear their stories of hope, and take them to heart as possible for ourselves.

Sanity may be an off-putting concept, until we think back on all the times we'd done the same thing over and over, each time expecting miraculously different results. We realize that this step involves transforming our perception of reality. We understand that following the program will mean leaving many of our egocentric behaviors behind and moving toward a higher, more spiritual existence. Step Two helps us envision this existence as being "restored to sanity," and in that statement we find hope for the future.

By the time we get to Step Three: *Made a decision to turn our will and our lives over to the care of God as we understood Him,* we are a little scared. We may think we've bitten off more than we can chew in this program. Perhaps we have no conception of a God or a Higher Power, never mind being ready to turn our lives over to it.

Then we re-read the step again and listen carefully in the

meeting as members share their thoughts. All we're really required to do here is to "make a decision," and that's not so hard. We have to consciously turn away from one path, which wasn't working for us anyway, and toward another.

As for "the God stuff," we think back to all the times we'd felt a presence of something greater than ourselves. Maybe we felt it when we walked into a meeting for the first time, and our Higher Power might be the group. Perhaps nature is the force that makes us think we are not alone in the universe. At the least, we can begin to conceive of something that is greater than our own egos, more powerful than our own minds—those are what helped us become sick in the first place.

The steps, of course, were written by white, middle-class American men almost 70 years ago. Most of these men were schooled in the Christian tradition and because of this, the steps refer to "God" and "Him," for better or for worse. But those of us who are different from these founding fathers, or who do not abide by any Christian tradition, can do what AA and EA members have been doing for years: extract the essence of the program while disregarding the cultural bias.

It's difficult but it is possible, particularly when you've reached your emotional bottom and are in need of help.

The concept that can be equally challenging is "turning

our will and lives over;" that old problem of powerlessness again. We are strong, independent people and we certainly don't need to *surrender* our will—we need to make it *stronger*—right?

Paradoxically, waving the white flag on our own willfulness is actually the first step toward becoming stronger. Until we admit that we've failed in our own battle to restore our emotional health, we cannot get better. Here we really come to realize that the steps are all ego-deflators, and for a very good reason: giving up our reliance on our self-centered ways is essential to our recovery.

After all this "work of the soul" is done, we may have the first of many spiritual awakenings in the EA program. We may have **faith** that the program can help us. Maybe we aren't able to spell out exactly what it all means, but then that's what faith is all about. It's about accepting the frightening nature of the unknown, yet believing that there's goodness there. These first three steps—involving admittance, belief, and decision-making—are the "surrendering steps" of the EA program, to which we'll return time and again.

We may put it off and put it off, but eventually we decide that to grow in the program we must embark on a fourth step: *Made a searching and fearless moral inventory of ourselves.* This step, combined with Steps Five, Six, and Seven, awakens our need for acceptance, awareness, and action. We start to see that this program might be a little more than we can handle on our own, and we begin to look around for a twelve-step person, counselor, or sponsor to help us out. We're either worried and afraid that this step will expose our souls, or we're looking forward to dumping the mental baggage that's been piling up for all these years.

Either way, **courage** will be necessary to continue down this path. If we haven't yet, we'll have to find where our courage lies and how we can tap into it. Perhaps we can't recall facing any change fearlessly, or maybe we've been so fearless as to be reckless in our past pursuits. Certainly the concept of a moral inventory is daunting for anyone. But there it is, the fourth step—can't get to the fifth without it. So just hold someone's hand and jump.

Sometimes it's helpful to think of our moral inventory as not so much a list of "the bad stuff" we've done during our lives, but as examples of mistaken thinking that led us to make poor decisions. The habits and attitudes that fostered those actions or resentments are being changed by the EA program. So really we're just taking out the garbage bags with the fourth step—the house is already being cleaned!

EA members say that the most important things to keep

in mind while doing your inventory include making sure you've done a strong first, second and third step; be honest and thorough; don't forget to balance each negative item with a positive item about yourself, and break down the time periods in your life or use one of the EA fourth step guides.

> When I did my first and so far only fourth step,
> I made a document in my computer called 'my
> life.' Then I started writing all I could think
> of. Then I would stop and come back to it later,
> adding pieces here and there as I came to
> think about them. I was thorough in describ-
> ing in detail the bad parts and trying hard to
> be honest, objective and not judging.
>
> *-Jakob*

We're now ready to admit *"to God, to ourselves and to another human being the exact nature of our wrongs"* in Step Five. In some ways, this step may be even more frightening than Step Four. It's bad enough to write the embarrassing details of our lives, but to *share* them with another person? That seems like going too far. And it is.

All of the steps go too far, past our own safe boundaries

where we've been hiding out for most of our lives. The reason for sharing this step in three ways—with ourselves, our Higher Power, and another human being—is to show complete **integrity** (commitment to a higher moral purpose) by breaking down each of those boundaries. Sharing with ourselves and our Higher Power are, at least, private. The third is painfully public, and we must choose carefully with whom to share our step.

But once that person is chosen and we have revealed ourselves, we understand why we must share it with another: We feel relief that we were not judged for the details of our past. We begin to trust that person, and at the same time we see patterns of past behavior that we identify as our defects of character. Perhaps for the first time, we look around the room at our meeting and begin to trust and accept each member for simply being the struggling, flawed human being that we all are. We have developed a kinship with God and man which will strengthen our resolve as we approach Steps Six and Seven.

This next step is a step of preparation: *Were entirely ready to have God remove all these defects of character.* What we must do here is develop the **willingness** to receive help in our quest for emotional wellness. That seems like a simple thing to do, because of course we want our defects taken away. But willingness can be tricky. It involves a change of heart and a letting go of our old ways that may become uncomfortable for us.

We find we are surrendering to powerlessness and shaping a new image of ourselves through these changes. Maybe we're not quite sure we like what we see, or perhaps we're finding it difficult to recognize our familiar attitudes and beliefs. It is no easy task to become willing to have our defects of character removed. What will we be like without our old "friends"—negative behaviors and stinking thinking?

Step Six is nothing if not a test of our emerging faith in something larger than our own ego, something powerful enough to catch us if we let go. That is the central question of this step: Do I continue to rage against myself, God, man, fate, bad luck, and destiny? Or have I experienced enough forgiveness, spiritual openness, and faith to let go?

Step Seven: *Humbly asked him to remove our shortcomings*, brings us face-to-face with our need to be loving and forgiving with ourselves. We find that it's very difficult to cultivate **humility** if we have poor self-esteem and associate humility with humiliation. Humility means feeling good enough about yourself to not have to embellish or brag about your life, or to hurt others by making them seem less thoughtful or intelligent than you. Humility involves honesty, self-acceptance, and openness to others, and many of us require a period of healing our own wounds in order to truly accomplish Step Seven.

This step also compels us to ask someone for something. As it happens, the "someone" is our invisible Higher Power, who can only be reached through prayer, meditation, and reflection. So we must develop a habit of this sort of communication in order to accomplish this step. Many people find it's helpful to spend a few moments in reflection first thing in the morning, asking God to remove our shortcomings. Others choose evening as a time to think back on the day, note any shortcomings, and ask our Higher Power for help overcoming them tomorrow.

Steps Eight and Nine are the amends steps of the program, in the sense that we begin to turn ourselves toward others we've hurt by our past behaviors. In Step Eight: *Made a list of all persons we had harmed, and became willing to make amends to them all*, we take **responsibility** for cleaning up the messes we made.

This is the step that takes many of us by surprise in EA. It's one thing to surrender to God, then review our lives and share the review with another, but to make plans to apologize to people and then consider going out and actually doing it—that seems crazy. That's why this step comes in the latter half of the program rather than near the beginning.

Steps Four and Eight are similar in that they are both about "cleaning our side of the fence." Often when we make lists like this a little voice in our heads is talking back to us. It's saying something like, "Don't put Aunt Martha on your amends list, even though you hurt her feelings last Thanksgiving. Remember all the mean things she did to you. She should apologize first!" Well, we're the only ones working this 12-step program, and the only person we can change is ourself.

What we're doing with Step 8 is starting to develop a healthy ego for ourselves and an accurate sense of ourselves in relation to others. Improving our relationships requires a realistic picture of ourselves and our past actions, so we again turn to our Fourth Step and note the names of people we wronged. Many may be unreachable, some may have passed away, and for others, our amends would do more harm than good. For these people, we write a sincere apology and then destroy it. Those who are still in our lives will go on another list.

This step only requires *making a list* and *becoming willing* to make amends. We are now familiar with the process of becoming willing since we've worked hard to cultivate a loving, trusting relationship with our Higher Power. So we put aside our fear, overcome the voices telling us that others were more at fault than us, and we forge ahead to Step Nine.

Made direct amends to such people wherever possible, except when to do so would injure them or others. The AA Big Book* is very specific about the benefits of this very difficult step. It says that as **justice** is served via the amends process, some or all of The Twelve Promises will come true for us. Just a few of those promises are: realizing a new freedom and happiness, not regretting the past or wishing to shut the door on it, comprehending the word "serenity" and knowing peace of mind, and realizing that God is doing for us what we could not do ourselves. Pretty heady stuff.

So with the enticement of such rewards, do we just go from house to house, mumbling "I'm sorry for everything I did to you," and call it a day? Nope!

In the 12-step programs, amends-making is a long and thoughtful process that sometimes culminates in our having to change the way we behave toward someone *for the rest of our life*. In other cases, a sincere apology may be enough, but it may not be accepted. We don't control the outcome of amends, but we do control the careful, spiritual way in which we make them. And having publicly vowed to change our

---

Alcoholics Anonymous

behaviors and attitudes, we move on.

Now that we've reached the tenth step, *Continued to take personal inventory and when we were wrong promptly admitted it,* we begin to understand how important it is to conduct our future affairs in a way that is not hurtful to ourselves or others. To do so is to accumulate a list of amends that will have to be made at some point. Instead, we take a moment each day to review our behavior, see if there is anyone we've harmed, and offer our apologies as soon as possible. If our own name is on this list, we'll have to spend some time being more gentle and accepting of ourselves. This daily task requires determination and **perseverance**.

These last three steps are often called the maintenance steps of the program. That's not to say, though, that we can coast our way through them. We have grown in maturity and tolerance in the program, and we now need to be vigilant about maintaining and deepening that growth or we will begin to "slip."

Many members find that if they haven't already done so, this step motivated them to begin keeping a daily journal or "feelings book." Such a journal not only helps jog our memory about amends that may need to be made, but it serves as a tool to increase our daily level of mindfulness. We don't want to fast-forward through our lives only to arrive at the end of the day not knowing quite what happened between breakfast and bedtime.

Mindfulness helps us slow down our days. We can then fully accept and let go of our emotions, and take time to make well-reasoned decisions. Even the *Just for Today*s point out that by simply and mindfully following the EA program, *I will save myself from two pests—hurry and indecision.* Often we find that just increasing our level of mindfulness limits the number of wrongs we will have to admit to at day's end.

We are now prepared to enter into a more mature relationship with our Higher Power through Step Eleven: *Sought through prayer and meditation to improve our conscious contact with God as we understood Him, praying only for knowledge of His will for us and the power to carry that out.*

Having paved the way for improved emotional health and wellness, we seek to enter into a dialogue with our Higher Power that will guide our days. The experience of a few minutes of silence—quieting our chattering minds for even a brief period—can deepen our **spiritual awareness**.

Many meditation techniques offer very simple instructions for finding a quiet place and focusing only on breathing in and out. Prayers—particularly prayers requesting direction in our lives or expressing gratitude for all we've been given—are also an effective way to discern our Higher Power's will for us. Both approaches are *listening techniques.*

We can no longer allow ourselves to be in a state of perpetual activity and talk because that's what made us sick in the first place. We must find that peaceful place within, and tap into the energy we so desperately need. We pay attention to our Higher Power's will for us, which is often just to live our everyday lives in a more mindful way. As we become better listeners, we notice that we are developing a source of spiritual intuition that will help guide us in times of stress. We may realize one of the most inspiring of the Twelve Promises: *We intuitively know how to handle situations which used to baffle us.*

We arrive gratefully at Step 12: *Having had a spiritual awakening as the result of these steps, we tried to carry this message and to practice these principles in all our affairs.* Perhaps we didn't feel any huge spiritual change and think the steps haven't worked for us. All we have to do then is to talk to someone who's known us a while, or to our sponsor. We will see that although our changes may have seemed small to us, they appear as a beacon of light and hope to others. Most of us will hear things like, "You look and act completely differently now," "Whatever you're doing, keep it up," and, perhaps from friends or coworkers, "Where can I go to get what you got?"

A spiritual awakening can be a grand, "peak experience," or it can be a quiet voice telling you that all is well. Many of us won't feel that sense of serenity all the time, or even most of the time, but we know it is there for us when we really need it. It's as if we were hollow before and now we have a tough, resilient core that we know nothing can damage; it is simply our soul. This is the message of Emotions Anonymous.

We can't rest on our laurels and keep that message to ourselves, however. This step is a step of **service**. You are called on to increase your involvement in your local meetings or on the Loop, to start a new group or to learn how to become a sponsor. You may even check into your local or national EA affiliates and see if you can put your talents to work.

This step also tells us to share the hope of the EA program with others, but don't feel that you must "bring others into the fold." Your life and your words are testimony to the strength of the program, you needn't feel that it's up to you to decide who needs EA, or even who will succeed in working through the steps. The efforts are ours, the results are God's. Our egos can no longer speak for us—our Higher Power does that now.

And how do we go about practicing these principles in all our affairs? This may not be as difficult as it sounds if we've truly taken the steps to heart. We are already being scrupulously honest in our dealings with ourselves and others, and making amends when we slip.

We are in the process of having many of our most annoying character defects removed. Meanwhile, we are asking someone greater than ourselves for direction in our life. This involves surrendering our will in all aspects of our daily lives—our relationships with our family members, business associates, and even our softball team or bowling league. That's when we know that the EA program has become a permanent part of us.

God, please help me let You guide me and
strengthen me as I live a new emotional way of life.
-Today, March 20

Interpreting the 12 Traditions

A tradition is a culturally accepted behavior that strengthens and unifies a community or group. For EA, the 12 Traditions are the guidelines by which our groups and our fellowship function. Our traditions are adapted from Alcoholics Anonymous, which began to see that such guidelines were needed less than a decade after the Twelve Steps were set out in book form in 1939. The book became an instant hit and hundreds of AA fellowships sprang up.

"The startling expansion brought with it very severe growing pains," according to Twelve Steps and Twelve Traditions. "Everywhere, there arose threatening questions of membership, money, personal relations, public relations, management of groups, clubs, and scores of other perplexities. It was out of this vast welter of explosive experience that AA's Twelve Traditions took form and were first published in 1946."*

The Traditions proved over the years to be an effective way of holding the fellowship (and individual groups) together without the need for more formal organization. They streamlined and simplified the sometimes-sticky issues of human relations that might otherwise have distracted members from recovery. They have since been adapted by EA and dozens of other 12-step organizations, and have withstood the test of time.

Sometimes it's helpful to review these guidelines as a way of making sure your EA group is functioning as it should. One way to do this is by purchasing a copy of EA's

_____

Twelve Steps and Twelve Traditions

publication *The Traditions* for your group. The information that follows is meant to supplement and expand on this publication, and help give us an even clearer understanding of the traditions.

Tradition One: Our common welfare should come first; personal recovery depends on EA unity.

The first tradition tells us that each member of EA is but a small part of a greater fellowship. Of course, our individual welfare is also a priority. But if the group that's helping us recover can't function, then we, too, will have trouble functioning.

This tradition stresses the importance of group (or Loop) membership and attendance as a key in working toward our emotional health. It also implies that EA members take responsibility for supporting not only their group, but also EA as a whole. This support can range from monetary donations to everyday services such as leading a meeting or making coffee, and will hopefully progress to a willingness to start a new group or to serve as an EA delegate or trustee.

The second half of the tradition mentions personal recovery. We must always remember that we come to EA for ourselves, not for another person. Perhaps concern for a loved one brought us through that door, but the twelve-step program is one of spiritual honesty and commitment that can only be worked by members bent on personal recovery.

Tradition Two: For our group purpose there is but one ultimate authority—a loving God as He may express Himself in our group conscience. Our leaders are but trusted servants; they do not govern.

Who ever heard of an organization with an invisible Higher Power as president? How would that ever work? The answer: It's the *only* way our organization will work.

Early on in the AA program, certain members became so well known for their step work that they were asked to take on positions of power in hospitals and community organizations. They were to set up "twelve-step wards" for those in need of recovery, sit on a board of directors, and draw a salary. This might have been the last we ever heard of the steps if things had gone that way.

As it happened, these members went to their groups to seek advice. Their groups told them in no uncertain terms that to "professionalize" a twelve-step program would be to eliminate the power it has to help the average person. EA works because we all take turns as trusted servants and no one has a standing rank or title. No one can become the official consultant for what is right or wrong in the program. We are meant to help each other recover under the direction—and only the direction—of our Higher Power.

It is from this tradition that AA, and sometimes EA, meeting leaders are referred to as the trusted servant for the meeting. It's important that this and the other tasks involved in running an EA group rotate among all members. Even those who start up new groups must quickly bring in others to share in the responsibilities and rewards of taking an active part in the group.

Tradition Three: The only requirement for EA membership is a desire to become well emotionally. The third tradition is very powerful. It tells EA members that they can remain in the program as long as they want to become well, not at the discretion of other members.

This eliminates any need for judging other members or evaluating whether or not they are working the program. In fact, members need not be working the program to be welcome in EA. Members do not have to share at meetings, donate when the "kitty" is passed, or be helpful or accommodating in any way to remain in our fellowship. This tradition truly brings home the realization that we are powerless over others, and that our lives, as well as theirs, are in the care of a loving Higher Power.

Tradition Four: Each group should be autonomous except in matters affecting other groups or EA as a whole. Every EA group can manage its affairs exactly as it pleases, except where EA as a whole is concerned. In that case, we must confer with our intergroup or EA International, since no single group has a right to make a decision that would affect the entire fellowship.

Autonomy gives each group the right to be wrong, to make mistakes, to correct those mistakes, and to feel confident that the group is working its program to the best of its ability. We are autonomous when we can move about freely and make our own independent choices.

Tradition Five: Each group has but one primary purpose—to carry its message to the person who still suffers from emotional problems. The mission of every EA group is the same: To reach out to others who are suffering. This tradition is important because it's also a key to every EA member's recovery. If we want to stay well, we must give away to newcomers what we've been given so generously through the program. Our egos may try to make us believe that our own EA group is different or unique, or has a higher purpose in the community. However, the highest purpose we can achieve is to be there when that newcomer walks through the door.

Tradition Six: An EA group ought never endorse, finance, or lend the EA name to any related facility or outside enterprise, lest problems of money, property and prestige divert us from our primary purpose.

Tradition Six tells us, "Keep it simple." It would be easy to make EA into a big business, endorsing home healthcare products or vitamins or certain types of psychotherapy, but that invites trouble. We are a loosely organized, extremely focused group that works best when we concentrate on helping those seeking emotional wellness.

For some of us, money, property, and prestige are among the many egocentric things that brought us to EA. Balancing the cares and concerns of the outside world, in addition to concentrating on being there for new EA members, is stretching our recovery, and our fellowship, too thin. Pursuing our primary purpose is our highest and best calling.

Tradition Seven: Every EA group ought to be fully self-supporting, declining outside contributions.

It follows that if we are not to lend our EA name to any outside enterprise to avoid conflict of interest, then we must also decline outside contributions. There's an old saying,

"He who pays the piper calls the tune." It means that outside donors contributing large sums of money might want some say in the running of our organization.

If large outside gifts and bequests were accepted, EA could someday be in the position of making difficult investment decisions, and feel obliged to support contributors in some way. Members would no longer believe that their donations and support were important to the group. We would lose that very important sense of being responsible, self-supporting, independent, and focused completely on our primary purpose.

EA does accept gifts from EA members, provided that these donations have no qualifications or requirements attached.

Tradition Eight: Emotions Anonymous should remain forever non-professional, but our service centers may employ special workers.

EA is a nonprofessional organization made up of dedicated volunteers and members. However, we do have a small paid staff to handle day-to-day affairs.

Paid staff members receive and administer donations from groups, create and distribute literature, respond to letters and emails, coordinate the Loop email network, assist in planning the annual convention, publish *The New*

Message, provide support to intergoups around the world, and perform other tasks too numerous to mention. In doing so, the staff carries out the policies determined by EA membership or the Board of Trustees.

Our nonprofessional status means that every EA member is equal—no one is an expert or paid consultant. Meetings are led by people just like you and me, since our experience of working the steps is invaluable. We can relax and share our experiences, strength, and hope with others.

Tradition Nine: EA, as such, ought never be organized; but we may create service boards or committees directly responsible to those they serve. EA International must function efficiently to provide a support system for our many groups around the world. But that doesn't mean we have an organized government that imposes rules and regulations on its members. Our government is our Higher Power. The boards, committees, and staff people of EA can only offer suggestions and support. They can help clarify parts of the program that are unclear and bring the EA message to others who seek emotional health.

Some committees coordinate outings, retreats, and other meetings that bring together our far-flung fellowship.

Others may serve as our collective "group conscience meeting," evaluating the health of EA as a whole and helping remove potential roadblocks to group unity. Committees and the Board of Trustees often rotate membership to ensure that many voices are heard. All those serving Emotions Anonymous must keep in mind that they are directly responsible to all EA members.

Tradition Ten: Emotions Anonymous has no opinion on outside issues, hence the EA name ought never be drawn into public controversy.

If our job is to become well emotionally and be there for others with the same desire, then there should be no place in our meetings for politics, medical, or religious discussions, or any similar issues. EA does not create position papers on local or world affairs. Our leaders are anonymous and our board and committees serve at our discretion. The only side we choose to be on is the side of serenity and recovery.

This atmosphere of calm and trust is cherished by many EA members. We know that no one will read from a religious text, compel us to identify our Higher Power, pass out literature for the latest mental health treatment, ask for political contributions, or in any way tarnish the EA name. Our lives are already littered with controversy and pain. EA is the one place where we can set all that aside and learn to let go and let God.

Tradition Eleven: Our public relations policy is based on attraction rather than promotion; we need always maintain personal anonymity at the level of press, radio and films.

EA's traditions and concepts make our program an attractive option for those struggling with emotional problems. But they can't attend a meeting if they don't know EA exists, or if they aren't sure where to find a meeting near them.

That's why this tradition tells us that it's okay to send out announcements to newspapers, mail flyers to local mental health agencies, or to respond (anonymously) if called on to participate in radio, television, or newspaper interviews. EA International even has preprinted forms and lists of guidelines and procedures to follow that can assist in these endeavors.

What we cannot do is promote our personalities and our personal opinions in an effort to make EA seem like the best and only source for serenity. We also do not compare our program with other methods of working toward emotional health. Self-seeking ideas and personal promotions do not fit with our traditions.

Our egos have already had plenty of fuel throughout our

lives. The 12 Steps all work on reducing our egos and turning our will over to the universal good. We can best be stewards of the steps by responsibly reaching out, in a spirit of love and self-sacrifice, to others who may not yet know of EA.

By the same token, it's important to consider that if EA saved our lives, how many more lives may hang in the balance? How many others could find hope through our program, if they only knew where to look? So we must not be reluctant to use networks and organizations such as clinics, health fairs, psychology conventions, and the like to get the word out. EA represents help and hope. Our job is to put out the facts and let others decide whether or not it's the program for them.

Tradition Twelve: Anonymity is the spiritual foundation of our traditions, ever reminding us to place principles before personalities.
This tradition saves the best for last: we're invited to soak in the atmosphere of love and acceptance that is created by anonymity. Anonymity is powerful because it is a great equalizer. It doesn't matter if you're a millionaire or a street sweeper—you are welcome. You won't be quizzed about who you are or what you've done. Your recovery is now in your own capable hands. With the help of others who also feel

protectively cloaked by anonymity, you will find recovery. No one will tell your family, your spouse, or your boss. You are safe here.

That concept of safety extends to our own egos. We are asked to conduct ourselves according to the principles of EA, not according to the principles of our demanding, needy selves. By placing our own self-seeking behaviors aside and embracing a common goal, we are setting the scene for our own growth to begin.

Help me find my quiet place.

-Today, May 29

Meditation Complements Twelve-Step Program

There are as many ways to meditate as there are ways to breathe, and probably five times as many meditation instructors. Meditation is an often-misunderstood practice that helps develop our focus, concentration, self-discipline, and connection with our spiritual nature. We learn to quiet ourselves, even in the midst of our very busy days, much as we learn to gain peace through the practice of the 12 Steps. It is a difficult skill because it involves learning to say *no* to our minds (which are always cluttering our heads with extraneous thoughts), and to our bodies (which strive mostly for comfort and satisfaction). Meditation is not some "hippie" activity that involves sitting cross-legged and wearing white robes and a turban. It is simply a process of turning our thoughts inward to focus on our spiritual energy. As we do this, we find we begin to align our will with the will of our Higher Power.

Most meditation instructors ask their students to spend at least half an hour a day in meditation, preferably in the early morning. Another half-hour is added in the evening as you become experienced. Veteran meditators practice for one hour each morning and evening. We who are new to this concept may choose to start with 10-minute intervals and work up to a full half-hour.

Another facet of meditation is repeating a phrase that will help turn your mind toward spiritual concepts. This is called your *mantra* (the form *mantram* is also commonly used), and it is said over and over during times of stress, during exercise, relaxation, or just before falling asleep. It is your cue to refocus your energies away from the rush of the moment and over to your Higher Power.

Many of us probably use the Serenity Prayer in just the same way a mantram is used. However, meditation experts recommend three traditional mantras which they claim have the most spiritual energy. These are the mantras used by the famous thinkers and leaders throughout history. The great spiritual advisor and political activist Mahatma Gandhi used the mantram *Rama,* which is simply a reference to joy in Hindustani. Others have used the words *Jesus* or *Hail Mary* as their traditional mantras. Each of these is short, easy to remember, and can focus our energies away from our earthly struggles and toward serenity and eternity.

The concept of meditation arose from the belief that discipline of the mind and body is necessary for us to achieve true freedom in our lives. If we are always **reacting** to our urges to eat non-nutritional foods, think negative thoughts, or do two or three things at once, we have very little free will to choose to **act** in more positive, productive ways.

Our consumer-oriented society has conditioned our minds and bodies to react, almost against our will, to pictures of juicy hamburgers, rich chocolate cake, a shiny, new car, or the most modern and beautiful clothes. We want to go to that new restaurant or even to those far-off beaches. The world around us tells us it's okay to focus only on our own needs—to give in to our addictions to work, sleep, exercise, sex, television, nicotine or caffeine, to gossip about our coworkers, or to vent our emotions by losing our tempers.

When we find we can't have what we want (and often even if we can), we become dispirited and let down. The experience didn't satisfy us the way we thought it would. Meditation is the ultimate dream vacation and gourmet feast all rolled into one. It is ultimately satisfying because it allows us to train our minds and bodies to be free of the impulses we've struggled with all our lives. No calories consumed, no money required. All you have to do is sit still in one spot and work on focusing your thoughts.

You may visit your local library or bookstore and ask for help in finding the extensive range of books on this subject, or you may prefer to use these simple meditation guidelines:*

1. Choose a spot where you will meditate daily. Make sure it is comfortable and not too warm or too cool.
2. Select a time for meditation and stick to it. The preferred times are early in the morning or just before bedtime.
3. Find a spiritual passage to meditate on. You will have to memorize this passage so that you can repeat it automatically. A good passage to start with is the Prayer of Saint Francis (see p. 67), although there are many other useful passages from other spiritual traditions. Your passage should be lengthy enough that you can concentrate on it, word by word, working up to a full half-hour.

---

*Meditation

4. Now you're ready to begin. Take a seat in your meditation spot. Sit upright, using good posture. Glance at the clock so you know at what time you began. Clear your mind for a moment and take a few deep breaths.

5. Create a picture in your mind of each word in your meditation passage, starting with the very first word. Focus on each word for at least 10 or 20 seconds, letting the meaning of the word sink in, then move on to the next. Do not allow your mind to interfere with this process by clamoring for attention. Allow yourself one or two of these concentration lapses, but the third time you lose focus, return to the beginning of the passage and start over. Feel yourself relaxing into the shape and pace of the words, feeling their meaning deep inside. Release the tension in your muscles. After what seems like 10 or 15 minutes (eventually working up to a half-hour or so), slowly open your eyes. Your daily meditation is now complete.

6. Decide on your mantra and practice saying it mentally to yourself throughout the day. You need not close your eyes, and do not practice this while driving or doing other activities where peak concentration is necessary. Let the mantra take you back to the feelings of relaxation and peace you experienced in meditation. Combining physical exercise with repetition of the

mantra is often a very effective way to let go of tension, particularly when practiced prior to an important event that will require your complete concentration.

As you move forward in your ability to focus your mind completely throughout your meditation sessions, you'll notice something strange happening. When you're tempted to pick up that cigarette, give in to hectic, hurried behavior, or dwell on the past, a little alarm will go off in your subconscious. You may begin to say your mantra automatically. This will take you back to the feelings of peace and relaxation you have cultivated by training your mind, rather than allowing your mind to train you.

You will find yourself tuning out your mind's and body's unreasonable demands and opting for a healthy choice, a positive word or thought, or a slowing down of your day to experience life's small pleasures. Your attention will be completely focused on each task you do; you'll no longer be as hurried, scattered, or forgetful. You'll be able to really "be there" for others in your life. You will have achieved a state of mindfulness that makes serenity well within your reach.

Prayer of St. Francis

Lord, make me an instrument of Thy peace.

Where there is hatred, let me sow love

Where there is injury, pardon

Where there is doubt, faith

Where there is despair, hope

Where there is darkness, light

Where there is sadness, joy

Master, grant that I may never seek

So much to be consoled as to console,

To be understood, as to understand,

To be loved as to love,

For it is in pardoning that we are pardoned,

In giving, that we receive

In dying, that we are born to eternal life.

Part III

The Power
of
Positive Talk

*Help me to remember that positive
thoughts and actions can improve feelings.*

-Today, September 13

Slogans We Use—What Do They Really Mean?

The world of advertising is great at rendering complex information into simple, catchy phrases that jog your memory when you're in a shopping mood. EA has its own set of short catchphrases—the slogans—that can help us when our moods, feelings and current situations threaten to overwhelm. Maybe it's time to take a closer look at these simple words and reflect on some of their deeper meanings.

Later in this chapter, we'll add to the list with new slogans submitted by EA members around the world.

*****

Let Go and Let God: There are so many times in our lives, sometimes many times every day, when we need to remind ourselves that although the efforts are ours, the results are our Higher Power's. We can't control the actions of our family members, the weather, our boss, the mortgage rates, the outcome of that operation. What we can do is be thoughtful, careful, and deliberate with regard to our health, jobs, family, and relationships, and to try to make the best decisions we can in our personal lives. Sometimes just letting go relieves the stress of our trying to control a certain situation and clears our minds to make better decisions. The unforeseeable future is ultimately in the hands of a caring Higher Power.

You Are Not Alone: We are born alone and we die alone, and there are times when aloneness, and even loneliness, is our constant companion, so how can this statement be true? It's true because as individuals, and as EA members, we are part of the human condition. We all share the same types of challenges, opportunities, and emotions, and we can be comforted in knowing that others are struggling also. Our Higher Power—whatever we believe that power to be—is spinning the universe and creating life. That power is ours to tap into for a sense of ourselves as a part of a great whole and for the sense that our lives are proceeding as they must. You are also literally not alone. Even in the seemingly endless "busyness" of the

21st century, the world is full of people who care. You can tap into that caring by reaching out just a little bit. Help others feel better about themselves by inviting them into your life, and lighting the dark corner of your loneliness.

One Day at a Time: Today is a gift. This day, this hour, this minute, this second is what we have to work with—no guarantees for tomorrow or the next day. Our job is to use this time wisely and well. We ask for our Higher Power's help in making it through this day in the best way we can, and we thank our Higher Power for each sunset. It helps to really look for the little miracles of our days, which can be as simple as a hug from a child, a blooming rose, and a car or computer that works when we need it. Of course, the future will not take care of itself, so we have to make some sensible plans for tomorrow. We have to plan for food, shelter, employment, education for our children, and retirement. We just don't have to live them at this moment, on this day. Today we live in the present and are grateful for the chance to do so.

Live and Let Live: Together with having only this day to live, we remind ourselves that we have only our own lives to live. We can **be there** for our friends, family and neighbors but we can't **be them.** They must make their own good or bad decisions and live with the results of those decisions, just as we must live to the best of our ability. If our self-esteem is based on being overly involved in the lives of others, we must re-examine our motives and perhaps reconsider our actions. By the same token, we don't try to make others' lives more difficult than they already are by judging them based on their race, religion, nationality, gender, parenting skills, or status in life. There is plenty of room in the world for all of us to peacefully coexist if we are fair, open-minded, and non-judgmental.

First Things First: With this one day, in this one life I've been given, I will be as good a person as I can be. I will figure out what is most necessary for me today. I'll do the most necessary things if I can, and save the rest for later. The first thing may be to work at getting myself out of bed and dressed; maybe that's a significant challenge some days. I will not make a huge "to do" list and rush around frantically trying to check off chores. I will be mindful of the gift of the day I've been given, and I will take care of my mental and physical health. If I work hard, I will also rest. I will try to live a balanced, centered life, because only then can I make good decisions. I will truly let myself feel—and then let go of— my whole range of daily emotions.

Look for the Good: Few situations in life, it seems, are as good as we hope or as bad as we fear. Every situation can be viewed in either a positive or negative light, and this will affect how we talk to ourselves and others. Positive self-talk will lift us up and allow us to see over and above a bad situation. Negative talk causes us to sink lower into our depressions, fears, and anxieties. And the good points of our current circumstances are not always obvious; we have to turn the situation over and around, finding out in the process how to fit these experiences into our perception of reality. Accepting this reality, and building on it in a positive way, is our challenge.

By the Grace of God: This slogan helps build my attitude of gratitude. By the grace of my Higher Power, I'm alive today. One more day to tackle the big, interesting, complex, painful, joyful thing that is life. "Grace" means unearned assistance and blessings from our Higher Power, but it can also include the concepts of mercy, pardon, or approval. We can't really **earn** our Higher Power's help and forgiveness because it is a gift freely given to us, but we can **live** it and make it real in our lives and the lives of those we love.

Know Yourself—Be Honest: The 12-step programs all require rigorous honesty. We must delve deep into our past experiences and feelings to come to know the person we are today. This is the hardest and most important part of the steps. Many of the self-destructive behaviors we practiced in the past, and perhaps continue to practice today, have resulted from being less than honest with ourselves. We tell ourselves little white lies such as, "I can let myself take that one drink because I've earned it," and, "It's okay to rage against my family because they deserve it." Rationalizing our behavior like this gives us permission to enjoy that second bag of cookies, that $1,000 shopping spree, or even to cheat, steal, or commit violent acts. These decisions are all taken from an attitude of self-pity and involve negative self-talk. We tell ourselves we can only fit in when we do act or feel a certain way. We say it's not our fault—it's the fault of our poor willpower, or the fault of other people driving us to behave badly. *In fact, our lives are in our own hands. People know us by our words, our choices and most of all, by our actions.* We can start living a new way of life right now. If the past is haunting us, the first, second, and third steps are pivotal, while the difficult fourth step allows us to clean the skeletons out of our closet and move on. EA gives us all the tools we need to come to know ourselves, love ourselves, and proceed honestly through our lives.

This Too Shall Pass: I can live through anything if I know it will only last this one second, then another . . . then another. Life can sometimes be like crossing a high bridge over a river. If you walk forward confidently with your eyes on your destination, you'll be fine; if you look down, you may panic. Our experience is that our feelings about certain situations do change over time. We aren't condemned to always begin sobbing when we think about a deceased loved one. We don't fly into a rage over a painful confrontation that occurred 10 years ago. Most of the conditions in our lives will change over time. Our unsolved problems are another matter, and may require a slightly different approach; but just as time changes our physical bodies, it subtly changes our feelings and perceptions of a situation **even if the situation itself does not change**. Our emotions are often greatly affected by our physical condition. If we find ourselves tired, hungry, and frustrated at the end of a long day, a new problem may seem insurmountable. We'll see things differently after dinner and a good night's rest.

I Need People: And people need me. I have unique gifts and talents that make me a valuable contributor to other people's lives, even if only in small ways. I have to be involved in the affairs of the world in order to be at my best. If I have social anxieties and phobias, I will try to get help for them. I will try to leave the house at least once each day, maybe just to say hello to a neighbor on the street, or I'll at least make a phone call to a friend or relative. I will try my best to get to at least one EA meeting a week. If there are no meetings near me, I will read some EA literature, call another member, or log onto my computer to post a share on the EA Loop. Fellowship is one of the most powerful healing forces of EA because it tells us we are not alone. We commit ourselves to reaching out for the help we need and sharing the help we can give.

Keep It Simple: Doesn't it seem like even the tiniest problems become complicated once we start to dwell on them? Our minds take over, probing for information that isn't there, attaching our emotions to each issue, and making problems seem more daunting than they are. The Serenity Prayer offers us a solution: "God grant me the serenity to **accept** the things I cannot change, the courage to **change** the things I can, the **wisdom to know the**

difference." We have two options—accept or change—when faced with a new challenge. We must call on our Higher Power for the wisdom to know the difference. If it's something we must accept, we simply turn it over to our Higher Power. If we must respond or change, we ask for the courage we need to pull apart the strands of the problem and take action on what we can. Life isn't easy, but it is often simple. Let's keep it that way.

I Have a Choice: This is the heart of the Emotions Anonymous program. We can always choose either to let our minds take us where we don't want to go, or to deny permission. It is always easy to fall into the trap of reliving emotionally charged situations, poor decisions, or self-destructive behaviors. In fact, in moments of weakness, illness or depression, these dark times seem almost seductive. We are still traveling that long road to self-acceptance, and sometimes it's just easier to let down our guard and go back to our old ways. It's simply what we know best. It is also what is most damaging to our self-esteem, our emotional health, and to our program. The challenge of EA is *to not regret the past or wish to shut the door on it.* It is an extremely difficult challenge, and we must ask for courage to do this every day.

****

Slogans Sent In by EA Members

EA members and others have generated a list of slogans that have helped them work toward serenity and peace of mind. Feel free to jot down your favorites and keep them in a handy spot for quick daily reference, or laminate selected sayings and distribute them at your next EA meeting!

AA stands for altered attitudes

Act as if

Action is the magic word

All discord is harmony not understood

Anger is one letter short of danger

Baby steps

But for the grace of God there go I

Clear your mind of can't

Do the next right thing

Don't quit —surrender

Don't analyze, utilize

Don't play the shame game

Easy does it . . . but do it!

EGO is Edging God Out

Expect a miracle

Fake it until you make it

FEAR (False Events Appearing Real)

Four A's—acceptance, awareness, action and attitude

Four Tools: journal (just write!), Loop (just type!), EA literature (just read!) and HP (just let go!)

Three F's—friends, family, faith

GOD—Good Orderly Direction

Great minds talk about ideas; small minds, things; average minds, people

HALT (Hungry, Angry, Lonely, Tired—warning signs)

Happiness (or self-esteem) is an inside job

HOW (Honesty, Open-mindedness, and Willingness)

How important is it?

I am becoming

I am not my illness

I can't, He can, I'll let Him

To wallow or not to wallow? That is the question

I want patience, and I want it NOW!

I'll know what I'm to know when I know it

If I want answers, I must ask questions

It remains to be seen

KISS (Keep It Simple, Silly)

Let it begin with me

Let it happen

Live in the present

Making no choice is a choice

Never trade what you **want the most** in life for what you

    want at the moment

No matter how wrong things seem to be, they are still all right

PACE (Positive Attitude Changes Everything)

Pain is inevitable, suffering is optional

Put it in the God box (write problems on a slip of paper and

    let them go)

Q-TIP (Quit Taking It Personally)

Reality: what a strange concept

Resentment allows *someone you don't like* to live in your

    head rent-free

Shed the "shoulds"

Step back; think

The happiest person of the lot is most content with what he's got

There is a God and I'm not it

Things I must do today: breathe in, breathe out

Use telephone therapy

Walk the talk

We can't direct the wind, but we can adjust the sails

What you allow, you create

When fear is near, sane thinking can disappear

When in doubt, don't

Where's the fire?

Will it matter 20 years from now?

Will power versus won't power

Would you rather be right or happy?

Ya gotta wanna!

You can expect a miracle, but you don't always get the
miracle you expect

You can only change yourself

*Help me to be aware of the location of the garbage dumps
in my life so I can pick and sort the fertilizer from the
junk.*

-Today, April 17

The Four Agreements and Four A's

The Four A's, *Acceptance, Awareness, Action, and
Attitude*, are tools we can use to help work through
specific problems or situations in our lives. For some of us,
the Four A's are familiar friends. Others are just
discovering the power of these four little words.

Much as we apply the Serenity Prayer to sort out an issue (Am I accepting what I cannot change? Am I lacking the courage to change what I can? How do I know the difference?), the Four A's can be used to determine what part of the problem is "ours," and what—if anything—we can do to help solve it.

Here's how the Four A's can be put to work on an example problem, such as, *Should I confront my daughter again on her lying about using drugs or alcohol? This has ended badly in the past.*

Acceptance: If we're facing a challenge that is bigger than us, acceptance almost always plays a part. There are some issues over which we have no control (birth, death), some over which we have very little control (other people's actions) and some over which we do have influence (our own behaviors).

The potentially explosive situation with our daughter will likely call for careful consideration and planning, and probably a decision to at least initiate a discussion. However, even when we must take some sort of action, we have to consciously leave the final results in the hands of our Higher Power.

Awareness: We allow ourselves to consider all aspects of a situation, even if we don't like what we see. Perhaps our relationship with our daughter has been scarred by mistrust or miscommunication in the past. Maybe we have confronted the problem in an angry or blaming manner, feeling as if she has let us down by her actions.

Most problems can be best dealt with by being aware of all of our emotions, including, most importantly, the love that is at the root of our concern. Also, we must ask ourselves if any of these statements apply to us:

Question 1	Have we knowingly caused any part of the problem?
Question 2	Have we been less than impeccable with our word?
Question 3	Did we take someone's statements personally?
Question 4	Are we making assumptions?

Action: We have figured out what portion of the problem is "ours," looked at the strong emotions that could sabotage our efforts, and now we're ready to brainstorm our approach.

We make a list of specific actions we might take in order to effectively communicate with our daughter. These actions must be thought through, and we may want to call on our sponsor or other program member as a compassionate and objective listener.

We select the best alternative—in this case, we decide to ask our daughter to lunch at her favorite restaurant as a neutral setting, after having planned a low-key, non-confrontational discussion—and we take action.

Attitude: Finally, we must adjust our attitude toward the issue we're facing. Sometimes our best efforts cannot change a tough situation. Sometimes we think we can fix the problem on our own when we actually need help. The attitude we take toward our problem-solving process often determines whether we learn from a situation or allow a negative outcome to weaken us.

Our talk with our daughter may result in yet another flare-up on her part, and we may then decide that a professional or family intervention is necessary. Or we may begin to establish a communications bridge where there was none before. Either way, our job is to feel we've let our program work through us to make us the kind of people we strive to be.

Throughout this process, we must remember to be compassionate toward ourselves. We are full of wounded places where we have been wronged and have wronged others. Our skewed perception of our world may have contributed to our flawed self-image.

But if allowed to dictate the course of our lives, our wounds and flaws will cause us to become sad, resentful, fearful people. We will always find ourselves seeking out comfort and healing, much like a toddler who's taken a fall, rather than taking responsibility for our actions.

Forgiving ourselves and others, and being thankful instead of resentful for our lot in life, allows us to begin to create a healthy new reality for ourselves. And from this attitude of gratitude, we can take a closer look at the "four questions" mentioned previously.

These are derived from a book called *The Four Agreements, A Practical Guide to Personal Freedom,* by Don Miguel Ruiz. An element of the EA program can be linked with each of the four agreements, helping us to apply our program more effectively in our day-to-day lives. The agreements and their accompanying program elements are:

1. Be impeccable with your word (*Know yourself, be honest*).
2. Don't take anything personally (*Self-seeking slips away*).
3. Don't make assumptions (*We do not judge, we do not criticize, we do not argue*).

4. Always do your best *(We realize that God is doing for us what we could not do ourselves).*

The first agreement is the most important one, and the one from which all the others flow. It implies that we speak with integrity, saying only what we mean. We avoid using words to speak against ourselves or gossip about others. We use the power of our word in the direction of truth and love.

The only way we can achieve this is by embracing the complete honesty of the EA program. We cannot say what we mean unless we can clearly see our limitations and mistakes, as well as our own positive attributes and strong points. We begin to know ourselves so well that our word is our bond. In this state of self-honesty, we are well equipped to make EA a way of life.

Agreement two tells us that nothing others do is *because of us.* What others say and do is a projection of their own desires and their own dreams.

How often have we had self-centered thoughts that our lives are difficult because others work at making them so? Most people are simply trying to get through the day, just like we are. When we distance ourselves from the judgments and opinions others, we can put our over-active imaginations on hold and begin to see what is real. Self-seeking becomes serenity-seeking.

The third agreement tells us to find the courage to ask questions, and to express what we really want. We must communicate with others as clearly as we can to avoid misunderstandings. With just this one agreement, we can completely transform our lives.

Do we choose to judge, criticize and argue, or do we make our decisions based on reasoned consideration? The former allows us to read our own selfish interests and assumptions into the actions of others. The latter requires us to test our own reading of a situation against reality.

The last agreement, *Always do your best*, is the trickiest. This statement implies that our best is not perfection; our best is the most concerted effort we can put forth at the time. The ability to do our best is going to change from moment to moment. It will be different when we are healthy, as opposed to sick; when we are down, instead of in good spirits. However, even if our "best" for the day is simply getting out of bed, our efforts will help us avoid self-judgment and regret.

Taking good care of our bodies, minds, and hearts fulfills the fourth agreement well. When we do so, we realize that we are deepening our sense of self-acceptance and love and embracing the principles of the program.

Many of us have spent so many years abusing ourselves and those we cared for that altering our way of life can seem impossible. And yet, as EA become a part of us, we realize that our Higher Power is working to change what we could not change on our own. We can now take the steps we need to truly do our best.

There are 12 such steps, and we just happen to have them at our fingertips. Let's take a look at some of the techniques we can use to make our climb a bit easier.

May I talk about myself in ways which are accepting.

-Today, March 18

Talking the Talk

Whether we realize it or not, effective and positive communication is one of the biggest challenges of our daily life. Not only do we often fail to ask the right questions or give the right information to others, we sometimes talk to *ourselves* disrespectfully. We judge ourselves and others harshly, perhaps slipping into gossip, criticism or pessimism. We assume we know what others want or need, and we act on these assumptions—sometimes causing painful situations that end in frustration, guilt, and resentment.

There is a way to slow down and think through the communication process, eliminating these roadblocks to serenity. We may find that this approach not only helps us avoid assumptions, but causes others to feel that we love, listen to, and respect them. In turn, we will begin to change our own self-talk to cultivate love and respect for ourselves. Our relationships with ourselves, others, and our Higher Power will improve.

Here are the steps toward clearer communication. Practice them often and they will come naturally to you. As you face each challenging situation in your life:

Take your time; think the issue through
Make a written list if necessary; Don't
    make assumptions; Be perfectly clear
Confirm that the other person/people involved
    understands the task or issue—ask for what you
    want; ask those "stupid" questions
Express your feelings in an appropriate manner
Stop yourself from slipping into negative attitudes and
    self-talk
Review the situation to see if you feel good about how it

was handled. If you do, celebrate your success; if you don't, make a note to approach it differently in the future. Then let it go.

Let's apply this approach in a relatively small, simple situation. Say your wife is making a trip to the grocery store to pick up some things you'll need to prepare a special dinner. You remember that you are on a tight budget, so you ask her to check her list. She replies, "You need canned tomatoes, pasta, lettuce, and dressing for salad, right? I'll be back soon." You agree, and two hours later, (after you've already made yourself a snack because you were starving and are no longer hungry for dinner) your wife returns.

You are already angry, but decide to ignore it and move on. Unpacking the bag, you see that your wife obviously made some other stops along the way, spending a lot of money on non-essentials. She also went to a grocery store you're unfamiliar with, one that doesn't carry the freshest vegetables or the top brands. The tomatoes are too firm to make a smooth sauce and the pasta is the wrong type. It takes forever to cook and becomes gluey.

Your wife comments that "you're not quite up to your usual gourmet self." You retaliate with a comment about her inability to stick to a budget; you both argue. You go to bed angry, telling yourself that your wife's attitudes are a real problem. You also berate yourself for a tasteless dinner. You curl up and fall asleep alone.

How could you have handled the situation differently, using the six guidelines above?

You would start by being perfectly clear about what you need. Make a list specifying brands, types, or stores; don't assume anything. Ask your wife what "soon" means to her and whether she has other stops to make. Even though you feel a little foolish, you tell your wife you're particularly hungry tonight and would really appreciate her prompt return. You remind her that extra purchases might be outside your family budget for right now.

She says she'll forego her other stops. You restate the agreement, if necessary, and thank her for understanding.

Dinner goes well, and you pat yourself on the back. You tell your wife how much you appreciate her being willing to do the shopping even when she's had a long day. You fall asleep hand in hand.

Okay, so life isn't really a trip to the store. But small things can often snowball into big things. When we take the right kind of action at the right time for the right reasons, we are living the principles of the EA program. Good communication that short-circuits assumptions, mind-reading, and "stuffed" feelings make our progress on the 12-step ladder so much easier.

Communicating with ourselves is obviously a crictical part of this process, and one way to improve our self-talk is to remind us that we are good, lovable people, and that prompt us to develop positive mental attitudes. Affirmations can also help us place our problems in perspective and focus on the what's really important in life.

EA members sent in many positive affirmations and thoughts, which may help us all along the path of positive self-talk. Repeat several of these while looking in the mirror each morning and see if you don't start to feel better:

Am I a human being or a human doing?

Am I enjoying or enduring?

Enjoyment is my way of keeping score.

God don't make junk.

Happiness is a journey, not a destination.

I accept all the different parts of me.

I am a person of high integrity and sincere purpose.

I am a unique, special person. There's no one else quite like me.

I am valuable, important, and worthy of the respect of others.

I am already worthwhile. I don't have to prove myself.

I am lovable.

I believe in my ability to succeed.

I believe in my capabilities and value the unique talents I can offer the world.

I can learn to live with unsolved problems.

I deserve the respect of others.

I deserve to be supported by those people who care for me.

I do most things easily and effortlessly.

I don't have time not to have time.

I fully accept and believe in myself just the way I am.

I have many good qualities.

I know what my values are; I am confident of the decisions I make.

I love myself just the way I am.

I receive assistance and cooperation from others.

I refuse to rush.

I take pride in what I've accomplished and look forward to my achievements.

I trust and respect myself; I am worthy of the respect of others.

I trust in my ability to succeed at my goals.

I'm optimistic about life. I look forward to new challenges.

It's good for me to take time for myself.

It's okay to think about what I need.

My body is the barometer of my feelings.

My feelings and needs are important.

My life is full.

My soul is part of the universe.

Other people like to be around me and like to hear what I have to say.

Others perceive me as a good and likable person.

Others recognize that I have a lot to offer.

Put it on your "not to do" list

Rest is the best reward.

Sip,don't gulp.

Slow is beautiful and powerful.

Stretch out the work, do less in more time.

Success is in the quality of the journey.

The more you take your time, the more time you have to take.

There is plenty of time to do what I need to do.

What I look like on the outside is not who I am on the inside.

When I take time, I make time.

When other people really get to know me, they like me.

The Power of Positive Talk

Part IV

When the Going
Gets Tough

PART IV—When the Going Gets Tough

*Give me the patience and tolerance to understand
someone else's, as well as my own, pace of growth.*

-Today, July 26

Members Share About the Program

Sometimes the most difficult part of the EA program is getting there, staying there, and being there for others. After all, how good have we been at making commitments and sticking to them in the past? How often do we feel totally comfortable reaching out to strangers? Do we look for excuses for not attending a meeting or neglecting our program because "we don't have time?" These are problems shared by many EA members.

> The toughest aspect of the EA program for me is
> that we have a lot of people coming and going;
> many stay only one night and decide it's not for
> them. I find it hard to share with strangers.
>
> *-Beverly*

The hardest part of the EA program for me is remembering that I need it. It's easy to remember when you hit gravel, and easy to forget during the smooth ride.

-*Yael*

Even getting motivated and dressed to go to a meeting is hard.

-*Kathy*

Forgiving ourselves, coming to grips with the cunning, baffling, and powerful nature of our illness, and learning to live with unsolved problems are roadblocks for some members; others channel most of their efforts into being nonjudgmental, and learning to trust other people as well as their Higher Power. There are no easy solutions, but the rewards are worth the effort.

The most inspirational part of the program for me is the progress I have made in handling my rage and gaining serenity.

-*Elliot*

The sharing and honesty of members allow me to be totally honest. Through this honesty, my spirituality has grown tremendously.

-Joan

I especially appreciate watching newcomers thaw out, recover and begin to move out into the world about them.

-Mark

Some of the legwork of the program has to do with changing our belief systems. This means allowing ourselves to let go and let God, accepting ourselves and others, and developing the discipline and determination to work the steps. The other half of the equation involves other people.

Dealing with the outside world by attending public meetings can be especially hard for those who have high social anxiety. After all, the wild cards are all there: members could become loud, abusive, emotional, or perhaps just confused and off track. Meeting leaders (called trusted servants) could have a bad day, and find it tough to keep meetings running smoothly. And how can we look into a stranger's heart—not just his or her face—and see someone whom our Higher Power loves and accepts, just like our HP loves and accepts us?

Being vulnerable enough to tell all my secrets to others is difficult.

-Ellen

The toughest part of the EA program for me is acceptance of others who come into the group with a multitude of issues. I have to remind myself that they may have difficulty accepting me, too. That act of humility helps.

-Dor

With constantly changing group dynamics, EA members struggle to become comfortable and confident in sharing not only their stories but the help and hope of the program with newcomers. Similarly, those who use the EA Loop as their home group may find it difficult to bare their souls to members they can't even see. They may become frustrated when others ramble or begin to violate the principles by giving advice. Loners who are working the program at or away from home without support of regular meetings or computer connections find that they have to develop their own innovative support systems.

Disciplining myself to use the tools is hard for me. I am sponsored by mail, which is very important in helping me feel that I am not alone.

-Kim

Finding and developing an honest relationship with a sponsor can be tricky, but members who have sponsors feel sponsorship deepens their program:

My sponsor is my inspiration. She works the program no matter what.

-Ellen

The lure of emotional well-being is strong enough to keep most of us coming back. But there are always those times when the *Just for Today*s and the Serenity Prayer don't seem like quite enough to pull us through. Then we turn to other people and other techniques to get out of the doldrums.

When I get 'stuck,' I call another member to talk it through.

-Kristan

My program is simple today: Surrender and gratitude work best for me. When I'm alone, I'm in bad company. I need to get to a meeting and get out of my head.

-John

What keeps me positive is reading the stories in the EA book, and writing different slogans or sayings in a notebook.

-Anonymous

EA members report that journaling daily, (particularly when they feel their program *isn't* working), is very important. Meditation is a powerful tool for some members, while prayer, exercise, service to the EA program, or spending time with a friend or sponsor can ease the way for others.

I've first learned to accept that bad days are okay. It is okay for me to cry, sleep, or feel bad for a few hours. Then I need to take inventory and look for the good. Usually I'm amazed at the positive things I can find in my "bad day!" Then I make a strong effort to *do one thing*. It may be to call a friend, go for a walk, or type an e-mail message to a loved one. That usually turns the tide. If not, I remember that tomorrow will be a new and better day.

-Dor

My most powerful tool is the prayer, *God grant me the grace to allow Thy will to be done, not my will.* I also rely heavily on the slogans, *One Day at a Time* and *Let go and let God.* I tell myself that if I want to have a pity party, I have to invite someone else to attend. If they don't enjoy it, then I'm not being a gracious host, and need to change the theme. That usually works for me!

-Sheryl

Many members mention that maintaining their serenity involves just that—daily maintenance. A morning routine of quiet reflection, or reading and a refocusing on the Twelve Steps, is an essential part of their lives. They realize that if they don't "lay the foundation," they can't expect to "build the house." They work at incorporating the steps and the *Just for Today*s into their lives, to the extent that their first response is an EA response.

When I get stuck I reach out for support from others. But if I don't do my own preparation before the day starts, I can actually drain those around me. I have to do my own footwork as well as fellowshipping and sharing the program with others.

-Mark

No matter what approach we use to energize our EA program, it is helpful to keep in mind that *this too shall pass.* Difficulties come and go as a natural part of life. Our job is to be as well-prepared and as resourceful as we can in meeting problems with a positive attitude. This usually means that we avoid focusing on the negative.

For example, new theories about raising children focus on *withdrawing energy from negative behaviors.* To withdraw energy means to deal with a situation calmly and competently. The parent who screams and yells—or reacts fearfully—when a child disobeys, only creates more chaos. The parent who quietly announces, "You broke the rules, go to your room for a timeout," avoids feeding the flames of rebellion. The problem is quickly corrected.

We can see this principle in action in our daily lives. Don't we often give loud, negative energy to the situations and people that trouble us? Do we sometimes throw caution to the wind and join the battle? When we withdraw negative energy, we calm an otherwise explosive situation. Fear and rage only fuel irrational thought; calm, reasoned responses set the stage for communication and problem-solving.

For some of us, throwing up a barrier of anger and fear is a default response programmed into us as children. Others move toward the opposite pole: stuffing their feelings, tuning out the controversy, curling up into a ball.

A key premise of EA is that emotions are neither good nor bad, they just are. The trap we can fall into is wallowing in these emotions. An emotional hangover such as this can trigger a downward spiral in our self-esteem and cause us to build up resentments toward others. We may sabotage our growth in the EA program, creating barriers to the successful completion of our fourth step *(made a searching and fearless moral inventory of ourselves).*

Rest assured, though, that we can begin to talk back to our feelings and our fears without falling into old habits. We can face anger, sadness, and grief courageously. We can learn to live with change and begin to turn over our unsolved problems. All we must do is learn the skills that EA teaches us. This is the message of hope echoed by our members around the world.

Help me to accept my feelings
without judging them or myself.

-Today, September 30

Don't Press the Panic Button: the Strong Emotions

An 11-year-old girl was acting out how she felt when she was overwhelmed. "I call it *when things go off the charts,*"* she said, spinning around wildly and finally collapsing in a heap on the floor.

That's exactly what happens inside each of us when we go off the charts emotionally. We expend a lot of energy getting dizzy and going nowhere. There are certain powerful emotions that can typically trigger this kind of reaction and have a strong impact on our self-esteem: worry, anxiety, panic, strong anger (or rage), and loneliness, sadness, and depression.

As we look at these, though, we must keep in mind that our feelings are meant to be experienced and accepted, not analyzed. Problems begin when we get stuck in these emotions and can't set aside our feelings to gain a more realistic perspective. Unrealistic perceptions can cause poor judgement and impair our decision-making.

It's also been said that some emotions are toxic for certain

---

*Brenna C.

people. This is not true. The emotions themselves are simply strong triggers; our actions in response to these emotions are what make them feel toxic. We *can* learn to act differently and refuse to allow these emotions to manage our lives. Emotions are not good or bad, but we can react to them in ways that are either healthy or unhealthy for us.

Worry, Anxiety, and Panic

What's the difference between the three? Worry is mental distress that comes from concern for something that's about to happen or is happening. Anxiety is a persistent sense of foreboding (or worrying all the time) that often causes side effects such as headaches, stomach aches, and muscle tension. Panic is sudden terror, and it usually includes the severe physical reactions of heavy sweating, increased pulse and heart rate, feelings of dizziness or suffocation, and a strong urge to escape.*

Worry, of course, is something we all experience. Sometimes it is a fleeting emotion that we feel in response to our own difficult circumstances, or a response to the actions of loved ones. Chronic anxiety and panic, however, fall into a category called anxiety disorders. They include social phobias and post-traumatic stress disorder. Anxiety

---

Overcoming Panic Disorder, A Woman's Guide

disorders are the most common mental illnesses in the United States, affecting more than 23 million Americans each year.* These illnesses are also linked to depression, agoraphobia, obsessive-compulsive disorder, and eating disorders, all of which can make our lives feel unmanageable.

There are dozens of good books about these issues and most of them stress the importance of ruling out physical causes for your anxiety symptoms. You may consult a specialist who would prescribe medication, if necessary; you may opt for practicing behavioral techniques such as deep breathing, progressive relaxation, visualization, and meditation. Some EA members practice turning over their anxieties by repeating the prayer referred to in the July 18 *Reflection For Today* (*Today* book): *I accept that I am having an anxiety attack* [or panic attack or compulsive thought], *and I surrender it to my Higher Power.*

Anger and Rage

Anger can be an extremely uncomfortable emotion. In some cases, we may have been taught not to express (or even allow ourselves to feel) anger in any way, and we are frightened of this emotion. Perhaps we came to realize the

---

Overcoming Panic Disorder, A Woman's Guide

old EA saying, *controlled emotions control me*, and began looking for help. We may have sunk deeply into depression, feelings of worthlessness, or self-pity.

In other cases, we may have linked anger with abusive words or actions aimed at ourselves or others. We might find it very difficult to choose a healthy, constructive response to this emotion. Or perhaps we've been treated unfairly and are enjoying our feelings of righteous anger—a guilty pleasure that will soon have us experiencing resentment.

EA tells us that anger is an emotion we can neither avoid nor nurture. We must find a balanced approach to anger that allows us feel it, express it appropriately, and then move on. Acting like a doormat or a bully are both poor responses. If we tend to be a doormat, we can change our approach by just recognizing and stating that we're feeling angry about a situation and need time to think how to respond. If we're the bully type, we don't have to follow through if our feelings dictate certain actions or negative comments.

The anger cycle may be broken simply by developing the honesty and self-knowledge that the program teaches us. Unrealistic expectations can feed anger, and we can work on this in our fourth step. In any case, if we're consistently experiencing that anger high—the burst of adrenaline that sometimes causes physical responses such as increased blood pressure and pulse—we should realize that we need help. There are many medical, psychological, and behavioral alternatives to taming our anger. And, as always, we will have the help of our program, our peers, and our Higher Power.

Rage is an extreme form of anger with uncontrolled, often violent, side effects. Because rage can have serious emotional and physical consequences for ourselves and/or those around us, we must seek out immediate help for this condition. *It's essential to call on emergency services or request medical intervention when you're feeling unsafe, and when you feel that others are unsafe being around you.*

Loneliness and Sadness

The endless cell-phoning and rushing about of the busy executive, and the sad reflections on the past of the older widow or widower, are two halves of a whole. They are both a matter of changed perception. We are so caught up in the emotions of the moment—whether that's the need to be better and do more, or the perceived emptiness of our days and our lives—that we can't see beyond them to any solution. Both imply that we are not good enough just as we are, and both can tend to make us feel lonely even when we are not alone. Both cycles can be broken by the simple action of stopping, stepping outside ourselves, looking at what's missing, and reaching out.

Loneliness can be particularly insidious because it sneaks up on us. As our mobility and health potentially decrease with age, our world can become smaller and smaller until one day, we look around and no one's there. Did they move? Most likely not. We just slowly pulled ourselves away, whether out of convenience or necessity.

This loneliness is then nourished when we feel that we are justified in drawing away from others. That can be followed by resentment or even anger that the others in our life no longer call or visit. The past can begin to seem more real and compelling than the present. We risk making the mistake of consigning our talents, thoughts, and feelings to a silent past. We focus on our regrets and losses, allowing sadness (which may or may not develop into depression) to take over.

The twelve-step programs are an antidote to this kind of loneliness. At their core is an emphasis on fellowship and support, a feeling that you are not really alone with your problems—your Higher Power is there to help you along the steps to emotional health. In EA, reaching out to others in your group is an integral part of recovery. You may ask for rides to meetings, make phone calls to your sponsor or other group members, or log onto the EA Loop.

It is when we feel most vulnerable that we come to realize that we are powerless over our emotions; our lives have become unmanageable. Step Two fills this void with the hope and promise of the EA program.

Of course, we can't make unsolved problems and health concerns go away. But we can do whatever is in our power to restore our appreciation for the beauty and complexity of life. No matter how rotten we feel, we can know that we have unique gifts to share. We must accept the challenge of continuing to pull ourselves up and out of our "trenches" of sadness and loneliness. We must also make a commitment to take care of our physical health by seeking treatment for medical problems, such as depression.

We can simply start by picking up the phone to call a doctor, a counselor, a friend, the EA Intergroup phone service, or the Service Center. If you haven't yet looked for EA meetings near you, this would be a good time to explore your options. Group contact people are always good sources of information about the EA program and how our meetings work. They will take the time to answer your questions and reduce your anxieties about attending a meeting.

One of the little miracles of daily life is that there are so many good people willing to help us in whatever way they can.

It feels good for them to help someone else, and it moves us one step closer to recovery.

Depression

Years and years ago, the average person thought that depression was synonymous with feeling a little down or blue. The cure was to pull yourself up by your bootstraps, put on a smile, and keep going. If this didn't work, you were judged to be weak-minded or weak-willed. Thank heavens science has redefined medical conditions such as depression!

Many depressions are now known to be caused by a deficit of certain chemicals in the brain,* treatable by medication and therapy in most cases. But that simple phrase doesn't begin to summarize all the emotions involved in depression.

When we are depressed we frequently lack energy but cannot sleep, become easily confused and overwhelmed, and have trouble with our concentration. We may find ourselves unable to cry, or unable to stop crying; we overeat, or lose our appetite completely. We might begin to have chronic physical symptoms such as upset stomach, headache, and skin tingling or numbness.

Depression has been compared to a huge, dark hole; a monster that's trying to swallow us; or, as Winston Churchill

---

Change Your Brain, Change Your Life

once said, "a big, black dog." It is so very frightening to face such feelings alone. But that is exactly why the EA fellowship exists—to take the "alone" out of the "feelings."

Emerging from depression can take some time, and not all medications work for all individuals. During this period, it's important for those suffering from depression to do their best to reach out to others—go to meetings, make phone calls, talk with their sponsors, or just take a walk in the neighborhood.

There may also be some steps we can take to speed the healing process. Scientific research points to a strong link between negative thoughts and physical responses.* The link has to do with certain chemicals emitted by our brains in response to our own thoughts. The solution? Do a little talking back. Learn to talk back to your negative automatic thoughts and feelings.

Writing these thoughts down can be helpful. Jot down the thought, then use a separate column to write a rational response to it.

For example, "My son is ruining my life," might be in column one. "My son is living his own life and I'm reacting in a way that's ruining mine," might be in column two. The simple act of writing helps make these thoughts seem less powerful and dangerous. Over time, talking back to your negative thoughts may become second nature to you.

Pretty soon, you're counteracting those negative thoughts

Be Your Happiest Self

with positives on a regular basis. Perhaps you can even begin to stop an unhelpful thought before it happens, substituting something positive. You are then releasing positive, instead of negative, brain chemicals. You might also try the "Boxes Approach" on the following page.

We can take charge of our own levels of emotional and mental health by doing what is in our power to do, and turning over what is not. Sometimes it's best to simply "rest" into a depression. This means allowing yourself to feel the depression, and giving these feelings permission to run their natural course. We can have confidence in our Higher Power that the depression will eventually end. We can relax, take a deep breath, and move on.

I thank You for the good which
will come with the changes in my life.

-Today, September 20

The Challenge of Change

Change can be a dirty word. We are usually forced into it and hope it doesn't kill us. We realize, begrudgingly, that we learned something from it, but we still try like heck to avoid it

The "Boxes" Approach to Negative Thinking

I. The Problem and the Feeling.
Your core problem surrounded by feeling about it

Maybe I'm in the wrong profession.	I have no savings —I'm scared.	My boss hates me.
I'm unattractive and unpopular.	**Problem:** **I am not doing well at a work project.**	I'm a failure!
My skills aren't being put to good use in this job.	I will be fired and become destitute.	All my friends are successful—why not me?

II. Re-thinking It.
In the middle box, put the most positive statement from above

My parents said they would lend me money.	Maybe I should try career counseling.	Last month I got a good evaluation.I won't be fired.
I'm turning it over to my Higher Power.	**My skills aren't being put to good use in this job.**	I have good solid skills in a number of areas.
Maybe I can ask Fred for help with the project?	I'm ready for a new challenge.	I am hard working and resourceful.

in the future.

The problem is that change is constantly sneaking up on us. If we don't have our eyes wide open, then surely it will surprise us once again. Why? Because we are always looking for comfort, instead of anticipating change. We adjust and readjust our appearance, our families, our homes, our jobs, and our possessions to make ourselves happy. Once we find a combination of factors that work for us, we want to wave a magic wand that stops time. Then we could enjoy our lives in a continuing state of contentment.

If this could ever happen, maybe 12-step programs wouldn't be as popular as they are now!

EA acknowledges that change is inevitable and, in fact, essential for growth. A key slogan captures this thought: *Just for today, I will try to adjust myself to what is and not force everything to adjust to my own desires.*

The phrase "my own desires" seems to summarize our problems with change. We don't always get what we want when we want it. We want to be healthy, and we end up in the hospital; we want to banish loneliness from our lives by finding love, and love lets us down; we want our emotions to be under our control, and yet we are powerless.

The longer we put off seeing that change is inevitable and can be dealt with, the more our worries and fears threaten us. Pretty soon it becomes so difficult to even leave the house that we begin to prefer our own suffering to any alternative that might offer help.

Change *can* be faced down and planned for, but it takes courage. Ask yourself: If you felt brave, what would you do today? Where would you go? Who would you meet? What kind of plans would you make? Would you be able to create a new reality for yourself that included being adaptable to change? Probably so.

Without change, there would have been no industrial progress in society. Wars would have continued without hope for peace, and scientists would never have developed innovative treatments for deadly illnesses. We, ourselves, would have remained suspended in our past.

The antidote to the stress that change brings is planning for the future, being flexible, and building our skills and resources to cope with the inevitable. We can apply this in our daily lives by having an open, inviting, loose attitude toward the little changes. If we avoid placing our everyday stresses into the category of "catastrophe," we have made a small step in the right direction.

Then we can begin thinking and writing out a few strategies for future, large changes. If your mother-in-law is becoming increasingly homebound, maybe now would be the time to come to terms with the thought of a nursing home. Perhaps your children will be heading off to college soon; what will you do to fill your days? Make a "Things to Think About" list that summarizes future challenges. Items on the list may include an upcoming move, retirement, healthcare issues, or money management.

Keeping our eyes open for potential change in this way truly allows us to become more adaptable people. Just this adjustment in attitude may bring us to the point where we feel less like a victim and more like a participant in our lives.

Higher Power, guide me to relationships
which will help me realize my potential.

-Today, May 21

Relationships and Boundaries

No matter how well we're working the program on our own, the true test of our strength in EA lies in working the program in our relationships. Our friends, family, children, boss, coworkers, spouse, or significant other can be the source of so much potential growth, awareness, acceptance, love—and pain, confusion, and anger, as well.

Relationships that foster respect and self-esteem are our goal, but the reality of our lives is often much messier. Perhaps we had poor relationship models in the past, or were sexually or emotionally abused as a child. We then have to learn new, healthy ways of being with others. We may have had addictions, compulsions, or mental health issues that prevented us from intimacy.

We've all had days when we've given and given, and have no more to give. Those are the days when our relationships suffer and feel unsatisfying. We're tempted to make snap judgements, or choices based on anger and resentment. We begin to feel that our relationships are broken beyond repair.

But the truth is that most relationships (other than those that are abusive or damaging in some way) can be repaired, or at least improved. The secret is to not lose sight of our own emotional stability and mental health. We have to have a reserve of serenity to be able to reach out to others from a position of strength, without losing our own identity. On the days we feel centered and "sane," having recharged our emotional batteries, we'll have the resources to deal with all the complexities of the relationships in our lives.

And they *are* complex. Intimacy and vulnerability are scary to begin with, but once you mix in other people's feelings and fears, you are wading into deep waters. Most people are not in EA or another 12-step program (although we're often convinced they should be); they don't take their inventory at the end of each day; they may not be living in a way that produces much happiness, and they don't know how to change. Their lives may be so unmanageable that they can only lash out in anger.

These people may be unable to accept or give love, honor commitments, be respectful, act responsibly, or be worthy of our trust. They may have an emotional or mental illness that they refuse to acknowledge. *And these same people may be our children, our parents, our siblings or our spouses.* We can't imagine life without them. We so desperately want to change them, but try as we might, we can only change ourselves.

At this point it's wise to step back and gain some perspective on the issue. We may have once been in the same place that our loved ones are in right now. Yet we have the program. If the EA program works for us, it does so because we are desperate for a new way of life, a way to make better choices and have more peace in our lives. Our past bad choices are acknowledged, but left in the past. We know we can only make the program work if we do it for ourselves, not for someone else.

The program sets up boundaries within us, like the clear walls of a plastic box, beyond which we compromise our own hard-won serenity. That serenity may be the only thing between us and loss of our sanity, or of our lives. And the decision to choose life and sanity over chaos, pain, and death is one we must all make.

We have made our choice for the kind of life we want to live. And we can, of course, reach out to help others. In the end, it comes down to a decision: Do I have the serenity to accept and learn to live with this difficult relationship, this unsolved problem, or must I move on without this relationship in my life?

Our values and perspectives change as we grow in the EA program. Often, we'll see the 12 promises start to become true in our own lives, particularly the 12th promise: *We realize that God is doing for us what we could not do ourselves.* Sometimes we just have to trust in a power greater than ourselves to resolve very difficult issues. We also come to realize that we haven't improved our lives on our own, that our Higher Power was with us each step of the way.

If we must find the courage necessary to make a change, or set up a boundary that will help us retain a measure of serenity, we won't be alone. We will have the help of a program that has guided us (and others like us) for decades, and the support of members who have freely chosen sanity, serenity, and life.

Help me remember that You and time are
my best friends in my struggle with grief.

-Today, August 3

Grief

Grief can seem like an actual place, a place where our mental presence is constantly required shortly after losing a loved one. Then, as time goes on, we feel compelled to go to that place a bit less often. And finally, perhaps long after our loss, we are able to make a conscious choice about whether to reenter the past or remain in the present.

Our grieving may seem so real that we could reach out and touch the person we miss. And, surprisingly, our grief may remain intense, clear, and powerful, even as the time we spend grieving decreases.

Grief is such an overwhelming emotion because it is a combination of so many emotions. Within the grieving process we encounter sadness, confusion, denial, anger, guilt, missing the physical presence of our loved one, and even questioning the spiritual nature of death and mortality. We may have had many unresolved issues with our loved one, which often makes the process tougher.

Grief may cause physical symptoms such as loss of concentration, sleeplessness or oversleeping, stomach and intestinal problems, and others. It is also difficult to find any sort of balance when we are grieving. We may isolate ourselves to be alone with our feelings, or we may want to have others around us constantly to avoid being immersed in our loss. Prolonged grief can even slowly slide us into depression, which may require medical intervention.

A wise person once said of grief, "There is no way around it but through it." We can't deny it, just as we can't deny any of our other emotions. We have to simply feel it, and then turn it over.

Keep in mind that you are not alone with your grief. You can and should try to seek help rather than suffering silently. There are many resources available to those who are grieving: books and literature (including EA's pamphlet *Grief*), and support groups, both in your community and online. EA members also can be counted on to reach out in fellowship when another member is going through a difficult time.

As hard as it is to believe, remember also that *this, too, shall pass.*

*May I remember that to gain my own
identity I must surrender my certainty.*

-Today, November 7

Growth and Forgiveness—Stuck in the Comfort Zone?

Remember the saying, "No pain no gain?" EA might modify that to read, "No discomfort, no progress." The truth is that growth is uncomfortable, as any child with growing pains can tell you. The alternative, though, is that we become cut off from potential sources of hope and strength. Our spirit begins to break.

There are many small ways to get on the path to growth again. Here are 12 ideas for keeping your spirit alive, well, and moving forward:

* Be a friend to someone who is friendless
* Make a call to someone you're concerned about
* Share love with someone who feels unloved
* Just listen to someone who needs to talk
* Sit with someone who is lonely
* Send a cheery card to someone who's having a rough time
* Comfort someone who's lost a loved one
* Share your experiences with someone who is confused

* Become more involved in your local EA fellowship; offer to lead one EA meeting, or volunteer for one job, even if you think you can't
* Spend a few minutes with a newcomer after the meeting, despite feeling like you don't know what to say
* Forgive yourself for one thing today
* Read up on and practice one new positive activity this month

In addition to these concrete actions, meditation and prayer are opportunities for self-awareness and growth. These reflective moments allow us to examine our own attitudes and beliefs. We may even discover issues that are holding us back from really working the EA program.

We might, for example, become aware that we are unable or unwilling to forgive ourselves for past wrongdoings. We could stumble upon old resentments that we still hold toward others. Both of these problems can delay or stop our growth in the EA program and point to a need to examine the concept of forgiveness.

The word forgiveness is an ancient Germanic word that originally meant to give or grant. The word changed over the years to reflect the idea of giving up resentments, as well as offering pardon for an offense. Today we consider forgiveness to *be our moral response to our own, or another person's, potentially immoral acts.*

Yet just this one simple word can conjure up a host of negative thoughts for us. We may think that we must *forget* or *deny* the offense we've forgiven. We could believe that we have to excuse the person who hurt us because, "It really wasn't their fault." We sometimes wrongly think that after we've forgiven someone, justice should be done; we should be compensated for being wronged.

In reality, forgiveness is a gift we freely give to ourselves or someone else with no expectation of anything in return. It is offering good will even though it was not earned or deserved in any way. Often it can involve forgiving an individual for committing an act, but not accepting or condoning the act itself. And, most importantly, *we do not have to love, like, or even know the person we forgive.*

Forgiveness can be one of the toughest steps we take in the EA program, but it is also the single most important step. The act of forgiveness releases us from years of resentments, opening us to new energy and growth. It is saying, "I can't, He can, I'll let Him," and turning a hurt completely over to our Higher Power. Forgiveness develops our own positive character assets, which allows us to work the program to the best of our ability.

Forgiveness can foster wonderful feelings of release, serenity, and hope, giving us the courage to face even the most difficult of the Twelve Steps. Also, forgiving others releases us to begin to truly forgive ourselves. We can let go of all the poor choices we've made, the abusive behaviors we've indulged in, or the difficulties we've caused for ourselves or our families. We realize that we are just as deserving of forgiveness as anyone else. We can make a fresh start.

Forgiveness definitely pulls us out of our comfort zone. There's nothing comforting about confronting the wrongs that were done to us, particularly those involving sexual abuse, physical/emotional cruelty, neglect, or violent crime. Like any opportunity for growth, however, forgiveness is well worth the risk. Hatred does nothing to the person we hate, but it can exact a terrible toll on our emotional lives.

We must try to find it in our hearts to forgive and move on. Our bodies do not live in the past; our minds cannot dwell on it either.

PART V

Progress, Not Perfection

PART V—Progress, Not Perfection

I give thanks for this day and bless every moment of it.

-Today, February 7

Take One *Just for Today* and Call Me in the Morning

When we first came into EA some of us wanted to know, "Where's the magic cure?" There had to be one, since most of the people sitting around us seemed functional, well adjusted, and even happy. They didn't seem to feel as bad as we felt, or look as depressed as we looked. Instead of a magic spell, we received information on the program and the unconditional support of others. But we needed more: step by step instructions for what to do when we got up the next morning. Here we did receive a bit of magic called the *Just for Today*s.

These 12 simple yet challenging statements can be our lifeline for a day and a guide for a lifetime. They work, EA members tell us, because they call us to perform single, positive actions that can immediately change the course of our day.

Some members read through and try to follow all the *Just for Today*s every day (a tough task). Some choose to work on one each day, and some select their special favorite to meditate on every morning. For newcomers, the power of these simple instructions can be astounding. And, as a sponsor once said to a new member who was feeling confused about the program, "All you have to do for right now is take one *Just for Today* and call me in the morning."

Here are the *Just for Today*s with some reflections on each:

I will try to live through this day only, not tackling all of my problems at once. I can do something at this moment that would discourage me if I had to continue it for a lifetime.

How often does my life present me with too much clutter, too many choices, overwhelming problems, not enough time? The first sentence of this *Just for Today* tells me that getting through the day is all I must do. If I feel up to it, I can take on a problem or a challenge, but if not, getting through the day is reward enough for my efforts.

The second sentence asks me to focus on one task at a time, without thinking too far ahead. If I actually considered the loads of laundry I must do in my lifetime, or the number of dark mornings I must get up to go to work before I retire, I might be tempted to stop making an effort.

This day offers me an opportunity to break down my life into manageable chunks. Today I will finish all my paperwork and have one less cigarette; no promises for tomorrow. Today I'll try not to yell at the kids. Today I'll go to my EA meeting. If I can do the right thing just once, *just for today*, and try not to project out to all the times I must repeat this action in order to be "perfect," I will truly have a magical day.

I will try to be happy, realizing that my happiness does not depend on what others do or say or what happens around me. Happiness is a result of being at peace with myself.

Trying to be happy may be an entirely new concept for us. Wishing or hoping for happiness is one thing, trying to achieve it by taking action is another. What stands in the way of my happiness? The nasty weather, the car that has to go to the shop, my needy family. But if happiness really comes from inside me, these negative events should just be a ripple on the surface of my serenity. Life will always have problems. The alternative (death) is not attractive. Living with problems will just have to be part of my plan.

Turning my will over to a Higher Power is a joyous thing and can create happiness. It won't mean I'll always get along with everyone in my life: that the cat won't get sick, or my job will always be there for me. But I can rise above these ever-present problems and choose to live in my happiness.

For, as the second half of this *Just for Today* points out, happiness is relatively simple. It is a result of being at peace with myself.

I will try to adjust myself to what is and not force everything to adjust to my own desires. I will accept my family, my friends, my business, my circumstances as they come. I will take care of my physical health; I will exercise my mind; I will read something spiritual.

Living in my head is my way to cope. I can easily wallow in the past or fast-forward to all the worries that the future holds. But adjusting myself to what actually is . . . that's difficult. I don't always like what I see. My family may be estranged or my health may not be what it used to be. I must be able to take a cold, hard look at reality.

I can't change many of the things about my life; I can't make everyone behave like I think they should behave. What I can do is cultivate gratitude for the gifts I've received in my life, and work at approaching problems with a positive attitude. If I see something I don't like about myself, I will develop a strategy to change it, just a little at a time. Mostly, I will learn to turn things over to my Higher Power and practice acceptance.

Our physical health is so often a reflection of our inner emotional turmoil. Yet I can take some simple steps to care for my body and mind, which are such wonderful gifts from my Higher Power. I must make an effort each day to take time for healthful meals, a good night's sleep, a walk. Since I must exercise my mind as well as my body, I'll also read one page from the EA book or another spiritual text every day. Or I'll practice 15 minutes of reflection, meditation, or prayer. I will promise myself to see a doctor or contact a counselor if I need this kind of help.

I will do somebody a good turn and not get found out. If anyone knows of it, it will not count. I will do at least one thing I don't want to do, and I will perform some small act of love for my neighbor.

The first two sentences of this *Just for Today* throw some EA members for a loop. What kind of good turn should I do, and how can I do it without being discovered?

Well, have I ever walked out into the street to rescue a

neighbor's garbage can? Thrown away old newspapers littering the park? Stayed late to finish a project, even though it wasn't technically part of my job? Simple actions like these show that I am taking care of my neighborhood and workplace.

When I refuse to draw attention to these acts, I create a secret pact between myself and my Higher Power. This can be a way to increase my self-esteem while avoiding feeding an over-active ego. I am a silent witness to the goodness surrounding me. I may also begin to see myself in a new light, developing more optimistic approaches to new challenges.

The third sentence is a bit mystifying, too. I do dozens of things I don't really want to do in the course of each day, don't I? If I am self-disciplined I do. But if I have given in to selfishness and self-pity, this may be a more formidable task. It may be tempting to slip back into old habits.

For example, it takes more time to sort and donate my old clothes to the poor rather than to dispose of them; it's more gratifying for me to gesture or yell at a poor driver than simply slow down and back off. No one will know if I don't send that sympathy card or don't come to work an hour early to help a coworker.

The path of least resistance is the path I usually want to take. Yet I often choose to do the more difficult task in the interest of performing small acts of love for my neighbor. These acts—as simple as a friendly smile during my morning walk and as daunting as donating bone marrow to a relative with cancer—foster sensitivity, generosity of spirit, and a certain mental discipline that I will need to face life's toughest challenges.

I will try to go out of my way to be kind to someone I meet. I will be considerate, talk low, and look as good as I can. I will not engage in unnecessary criticism or finding fault, nor try to improve or regulate anybody except myself.

Just for Today number six can seem almost overwhelming, especially to the newcomer. Not only am I to look my best and be kind to others, I'm supposed to avoid gossip and criticism and replace judgmental behavior with acceptance. This is a very tall order.

But the *Just for Today*s do build on one another. In number three, I learn that I can only change myself; in four, I decide to take better care of myself physically and mentally; number five asks me to nurture kindness and compassion.

Now I just blend all these skills together and add a dash of prudence. I will not gossip about, criticize, or try to control others. This is easier said than done. But as my self-esteem grows, my need to belittle and manipulate others will naturally decrease.

My Higher Power accepts me just as I am. If I am cherished in this way, then so are my family members, neighbors, and everyone else I come in contact with. Just for this one day, anything is possible.

I will have a program. I may not follow it exactly, but I will have it. I will save myself from two pests—hurry and indecision.

I can cling to this *Just for Today* when all the others seem out of reach. It simply says that I recognize that I'm in a twelve-step program. This program holds out the promise of serenity in return for my hard work and honesty. I will think about this during the day, even if I'm not directly working the steps.

Strangely enough, as this thought becomes part of me, I'll find that I'm less likely to rush through my day and be overwhelmed by the smallest decisions. I'll become mindful of my need for serenity. That in itself is a big step toward having a better day.

I will stop saying, "If I had time." I never will find time for anything. If I want time, I must take it.

Much of the EA program has to do with carefully using my time. I am given this day only, and I must live it with mindfulness and gratitude. This implies that I will decide which goals are most important to me, and make progress toward achieving them. Other "busyness" in my life will have to wait.

I have only 24 hours, and some of those must be set aside for work, meals, exercise, prayer/meditation, and sleep. The few hours left must be jealously guarded and used only to bring my life more in accord with the will of my Higher Power.

This can be as small a thing as reading to my children before bedtime each night, or as great a thing as completing a college degree to pursue the job of my dreams. I will practice saying *no* to activities that I don't have time for and *yes* to more of the joys of this life.

I will have a quiet time of meditation wherein I shall think of my Higher Power, of myself, and of my neighbor. I shall relax and seek truth.

The sentence *I shall relax and seek truth* often jumps out at newcomers. What is this, a philosophy seminar? A yoga class? No. It's a program that teaches me to live as if I know that I can't live forever. I will honor my commitment to EA by getting in touch with my feelings about life, love, loss, and a power greater than myself. I will seek out those truths that transcend my daily hopes and fears.

I will become more than a "human doing"; I'll realize my potential to be a "human being." To do that I must stop being busy, and start thinking, praying, and meditating.

What do I think, pray or meditate about? My Higher Power, myself, my program, my loved ones. And I will listen for a little voice inside that distinguishes truth from falsehood; the will of my Higher Power from my will.

I might use guided imagery, music, or EA literature during this reflection time. Or I may want to commit to a daily half-hour of traditional meditation (see page xx). Even if I just relax, shut my eyes, and briefly reflect on my day, I can reconnect with the spiritual energy that is so important to working my program.

I shall be unafraid. Particularly, I shall be unafraid to be happy, to enjoy what is good, what is beautiful, and what is lovely in life.

Telling me to be unafraid can be like telling me to win the lottery—it seems impossible. Fear has motivated so many of my actions and decisions, and has been the cause of so much anxiety. But the EA program challenges all of my old beliefs, assumptions, and behaviors, so perhaps it is even strong enough to help me fight off fear.

The first step toward battling my fearfulness is to focus on a day when things seem to be going my way. I am positive, energetic and hopeful. I am feeling at one with the will of my Higher Power.

Then, when that first shadow of fear approaches, I can fight back by recalling the good feelings I enjoyed on that special day. I will stay positive by reaching for my affirmations, such as FEAR is False Events Appearing Real; I can't, He can, I'll let Him; God don't make junk; and others (see pages 80, 94).

If I can keep my fears at bay for even a little while, I'll begin to build the confidence I need to acknowledge, and then let go of, my fear. I know that reprogramming my fear response will take time. I will celebrate the small victories, which tell me that there is hope.

So much is good and beautiful in the world around me. I will try to open myself to this goodness and refuse to let my fears run my life.

I will not compare myself with others. I will accept myself and live to the best of my ability.

This *Just for Today* asks me to look at my self-esteem

level. Do I feel good enough about myself to avoid comparing and judging? Or, if I'm still prone to viewing myself through the eyes of others, can I learn to love myself just as I am?

After all, other people are not what they appear to be. Everyone has their problems and flaws underneath their mask of "normalcy," so my comparisons would be inaccurate anyway. If I must compare, I'll compare myself with my Higher Power's wishes for me: How would my loving Higher Power want me to feel about myself? What steps can I take to respect myself as much as my Higher Power respects me? What would my Higher Power want me to do today?

Most likely, my Higher Power simply wants me to choose to believe in myself, to believe that I can live this one day. Following the will of my Higher Power is so often just doing the ordinary things I do every day but with a sense of gratitude.

Suicidal thoughts or depression may make it tempting for me to go back to bed and pull the covers over my head. But I now have some tools to use when these feelings overwhelm me. The *Just for Todays* are only one of the many tools I can use to build a new way of life through the 12-step program of Emotions Anonymous.

Grant me the courage to take an honest look at myself.

-Today, April 12

Fourth/Tenth Step Guides and Worksheets

Step Four

How many people do you know who have taken stock of their lives, written down all their strengths and liabilities, and come to terms with making amends? Unless they're 12-step program members, the number is likely close to zero. It's just not a popular pastime to analyze one's life and then commit to changing it. It's not fun, it's not easy, and while the Fourth Step is necessary and satisfying, it usually doesn't provide the immediate gratification that our society has conditioned us to desire.

So why do we Twelve Steps folks take on the fourth step? Most of us must do it to save our lives. We also want to be able to say that we are living the type of life that makes us proud of ourselves.

The fourth step separates the "men from the boys, and the women from the girls." It is the step that newcomers usually fear most and one that should not be taken lightly. But it is the first tangible result of our commitment to the EA program. The benefits of doing this step honestly and completely are immeasurable.

Part of the problem with the fourth step is that we aren't given direct, step-by-step instructions on how to complete it. This is because everyone must decide what type of system works for them. However, EA literature does provide helpful guidance on this step (including the material in the *Step by Step* book). Other Twelve Step programs offer interesting fourth step approaches as well.

Following is an outline of several methods you may consider using to complete this step. Feel free to choose one that works best for you or make up your own.

Rate Your Assets and Defects

This fourth step approach asks questions that can help you narrow down your key character traits. Place a number from one to 10 in the spaces below. One indicates you have very low levels of this attribute, five shows you act in this way a moderate amount of the time, and 10 indicates a high level of this attribute. If you have never shown this characteristic, place a zero on the line.

On a separate sheet of paper, note your five "highest-scoring" assets and defects. Then write a little (or a lot) about each, going back as far into your past as you can remember. Make sure you give concrete examples of every time these feelings or characteristics caused difficulty in your life. You may choose to work on the lower-scoring defects as you progress in the program.

Don't forget to celebrate your good qualities! Keep in mind, too, that weaknesses often possess the building blocks of strengths—for example, if you're a daredevil, you probably also have a great zest for life. You can salvage that good quality and work on changing only the high-risk behavior.

Am I, or Have I Been in the Past . . .

A good judge of character?___

A good communicator?___

A good decision-maker?___A good planner?___

A hard worker?___

A person who has a zest for life?___

A person who takes care of physical health?___

A person with good self-esteem?___

A volunteer who contributes to the community?___

Able to do one thing at a time?___

Able to laugh at myself?___

Able to live in the moment?___

Able to live one day at a time?___

Able to stand up for myself?___

Able to stop and smell the roses?___

Accepting of others?___

Accepting of myself?___

Aware of my own self-worth?___

Calm?___

Careful in my life and work?___

Cheerful?___

Compassionate?___

Confident?___

Considerate of others?___

Curious?___

Creative?___

Detail-oriented?___

Easygoing? ___

Energetic?___

Enjoyable to be around?___

Enthusiastic?___

Experiencing a healthy range of emotions?___

Friendly?___

Flexible?___

Fun?___

Generous?___

Gentle?___

Good-natured?___

Good at expressing my feelings?___

Good at forgiving myself?___

Good at forgiving other people?___

Helpful?___

Honest with myself?___

Honest with others?___

Hopeful?___

Humorous?___

Humble?___

Intelligent?___

Kind?___

Loving?___

Moderate in the areas of food, drink, sexual matters and so
   forth?___

Neat in appearance?___

Open-minded?____

Optimistic? ___

Organized?___

Outgoing?___

Patient?___

Perceptive?___

Polite?___

Punctual?___

Realistic?___

Relaxed?___

Reliable?___

Responsible___

Sincere?___

Soft-spoken?___

Spontaneous?___

Thankful for my blessings?___

Thoughtful?___

Tolerant?___

Trusting?___

Trustworthy?___

Using the talents my Higher Power gave me?___

Unselfish?___

Am I, Or Have I Been in the Past...

A "catastrophizer" (make everything seem worse than it is)?___

A complainer? ___

A daredevil?___

A gossip?___

A hypochondriac (always thinking I'm sick)?___

A perfectionist?___A worrywart?___

**A person who abuses others physically or emotionally?___

** A person who abuses substances?___

** A person who doesn't want to go on living?___

A person who lives in the past?___

A person who shuts the door on the past?___

A workaholic?___

An "all or nothing" type of person?___

Always feeling driven, compulsive or on fast-forward?___

Always late?___

Always over- or under-estimating myself?___

Always over- or under-estimating others?___

*Angry ?___

Anxious or tense?___

Apathetic?___

Carrying a great deal of guilt?___

Controlling?___

Cruel or unkind?___

Defensive?___

Despondent (without hope)?___

*Dishonest with myself?___

*Dishonest with others?___

Disorganized?___

Fearful?___

Gloomy?___

Hypocritical?___

Ill-tempered?___

Impatient?___

Impulsive?___

Intolerant?___

Irresponsible?___

Jealous?___

Lazy?___

Living in my own head?___

Loud?___

Mistake-or accident-prone?

Obsessed with my own actions or problems?___

Overly critical of myself?___

Overly critical of others?___

Overly dependent on others?___

Overly dramatic?___

Overly emotional?___

Overly worried about others?___

Overly talkative or hyperactive?___

Oversensitive?___

Procrastinating?___

**Rageful?___

Regretful?___

Resentful?___

Rigid?___

Rude?___

Selfish?___

Self-righteous?___

Slovenly (don't take care of appearance)?___

Smug?___

Someone who blames others?___

Someone who can't say no?___

Someone who gives too much?___

Someone who holds a grudge?___

Someone with poor self-esteem?___

Stubborn?___

Sullen?___

Suspicious?___

Unable to "feel" my feelings?___

Undisciplined?___

Ungrateful?___

Unwilling to seek help when I need it?___

**Very depressed?___

*Withdrawn from others, unable to leave the house?___

Wasteful?___

*These areas will need special attention in order for you to
successfully work the EA program.*

** *If these areas are checked and you aren't receiving professional help for them, you should seek help immediately.*

Inspired by a *Fourth Step Inventory Guide*, copyright 1980, Emotions Anonymous. Currently out of print.

Make a List

This worksheet allows you to address one character defect at a time, and trace its origins back to your past. You will also begin to think about the people in your life (including yourself) who are deserving of amends.

List a character defect that is causing me pain or unhappiness:_____

Give specific examples from my past of how this defect has resulted in behaviors that have caused difficulty for me or others? _____

Whom have I hurt (including myself) by this behavior?_____

How can changing this behavior improve my relationship with others, or increase my own self-esteem?

_____

How can I start to change this behavior?

_____

Which character assets am I most proud of?

_____

Inspired by *My Personal Inventory: My Strengths and Limitations,* copyright 1994, Emotions Anonymous.

Chart Your Course

This fourth step guide focuses your attention on five categories that may have heavily contributed to forming your character.

Answer each question honestly, going as far back as you can remember, to create your chart. You will end up with five separate sheets of paper that are, in essence, your fourth step. Keep in mind that your job now is to identify your character strengths and weaknesses. You need not solve any problems or take any significant action at this point.

My Past—What Made Me Who I Am Today?

<u>Column 1</u>	<u>Column 2</u>	<u>Column 3</u>
Name an incident that shaped my life.	*Was I at fault for any of it?*	*Who needs amends?*
1. I was bullied on the playground.	No—except I never told anyone or asked for help.	Me
2. _____	_____	_____

My Positive Characteristics—Which Strengths Can I Build On?

<u>Column 1</u>	<u>Column 2</u>	<u>Column 3</u>
Name an example of how I responded well to a difficult situation?	*What positive characteristics does this illustrate?*	*Can I use this asset to work the 12 Steps? How?*
1. I stood up to my parents to protect my sister.	Courage	Yes. Face 4th/5th steps.
2. _____	_____	_____

My Fears—How Have They Changed Me?

Column 1	Column 2	Column 3
Name one thing that makes me fearful.	*What is my response?*	*How does this affect me?*
1. Being with strangers.	I don't go anywhere.	I am lonely.
2. _____	_____	_____

My Resentments—How Do They Harm Me?

Column 1	Column 2	Column 3
Name one person, institution, or principle toward which I feel resentment?	*Why?*	*How does this affect me?*
1. I resent my wife.	She is always nagging me.	I am unhappy at home.
2. _____	_____	_____

My Sexual Conduct—How Have I Hurt Others or Myself?

<u>Column 1</u>	<u>Column 2</u>	<u>Column 3</u>
Name a sexual incident that made me or my partner(s) fell uncomfortable?	*What caused the uncomfortable feelings?*	*How has this affected me or others?*
1. I was not up front about having a sexually transmitted disease (STD).	I was being dishonest.	I feel guilty; may have passed on the STD.
2. _____	_____	_____

Inspired by the *AA Big Book*, copyright 1939, Alcoholics Anonymous.

Step Ten

Step Four may be just a memory now, if you've been in Emotions Anonymous for a long time. Or perhaps you've been in a number of twelve-step programs and have completed several fourth steps. Maybe you've even decided to do this important step every few years, as the circumstances of your life change.

In any case, the tenth step asks us to maintain what we've accomplished in our Fourth Step by *cleaning our side of the fence* on a daily basis. This can be a challenge, but it is also an opportunity for new growth.

Some of us choose to write in a journal each evening, listing the positive and negative things that have happened during the day, and noting any amends that we will need to make. Others evaluate their day during prayer or meditation. And still others prefer to use a tool, such as EA's *Spot Check Inventory.*

Here is an expanded version of the Spot Check, followed by some questions we may use to guide our daily reflections.

Check all that apply:

Today I was . . .	**Today I was . . .**
Angry __	Slow to anger __
Critical __	Accepting __
Lonely __	Feeling loved __
A complainer__	A positive person __
Fearful __	Courageous __
Resentful __	Forgiving __
Self-centered __	Considerate of others __
Impulsive and self-indulgent __	Self-disciplined __
Impatient __	Generous with my time __
Negative __	Optimistic and hopeful __
Stubborn __	Willing to compromise __

Ignoring the needs of my body __ Taking care of my physical health __

Forcing my own will into being __ Turning my will over to the care of my Higher Power __

Answer each question as honestly as possible:

1. Was I the best person I could be today, taking into account all the circumstances of my life? Why or why not?
2. Was I as considerate of others as I should have been?
3. Was I able to put aside the petty annoyances of my day and see the good and the beautiful things in life?
3. Was I able to apologize when I wronged someone?
4. Do I owe amends to myself or others for actions I have taken today?
5. How will I go about making these amends?

Be my rain gear to get me through the storms I face.

-Today, January 22

The Integrity of the Group: Mediating Conflict

All 12-step programs, and in fact all support groups without a facilitator, face the same kinds of opportunities and problems. The opportunity is there for a group of strangers to come together around a single goal, increase emotional health, and help each other without the presence of a professional. This is a very important opportunity, because it draws on the strengths of regular individuals experiencing common difficulties. In the absence of a single leader, the group must decide how to conduct itself in a way that is most helpful for everyone.

The potential problems, however, can be very difficult to face and solve. They fall into four categories: problems with common purpose, structure, behavior, and function.

All groups have to discern their **common purpose**, whether it's retired gentlemen going out for coffee to socialize, or EA groups trying to help members become well emotionally. The common purpose sets the tone and "membership requirements" for the group.

A person who attends EA for the sole purpose of distributing religious literature, or meeting a potential mate, does not fit with the group's common purpose. This person can be asked to leave. (However, sometimes people think they're attending for one purpose, and end up staying for quite another purpose. So EA groups will often invite these people to attend a few meetings.) The existence of a common purpose allows an EA group to hold group conscience meetings, which spell out acceptable group behavior and address other issues of concern.

The **structure** of groups can be either informal or formal. The men going out for coffee are obviously an informal group. They can vary their meeting times to suit the membership. They don't have to worry about behavior guidelines, since their group is not open to the public.

EA groups do have set meeting days and times, because our meetings are open to the public. Our fellowship does have a formal suggested meeting format, as well as Twelve Concepts and Twelve Traditions that explain our group procedures and guidelines.

The advantage of following a formal meeting format is that members, no matter where they're from, feel comfortable attending any EA group. Newcomers are comforted by the sense of structure and certainty. The format is designed to be read aloud, so that anyone can lead the meeting as its trusted servant. The experience of leading a meeting can be powerful, particularly for newer members; just this simple action can increase one's commitment to the EA program.

The next element, **behavior**, causes most of the serious problems that groups experience. The EA pamphlet *Maintaining Group Serenity* outlines meeting behavior problems ranging from interruptions, crosstalk, and advice-giving, to inappropriate discussions about religious or political issues. Even a member whose "shares" are lengthy and off-topic can disrupt the flow of the meeting. In fact, EA members around the world tell us that meeting disruption is one of their most worrisome areas of concern.

In dealing with group behavior, keep in mind that each member has a hand in the success of EA meetings. We must all learn to respond appropriately to disruptive members, and get the meeting back on track. If we always refer behavior problems to the trusted servant, or to the person who started the meeting, we are entrusting too much power to that person. Anger and resentment may follow.

Some EA groups find that posting an easy-to-read list of EA's traditions and concepts on the meeting table empowers members to speak up. For example, a member could simply say, "Excuse me, I feel uncomfortable because I think we are violating Tradition ___," and ask to read that tradition or concept.

It is important to explain the difference between appropriate and inappropriate behavior. Sometimes this can be done by one or two members talking to the person outside the meeting in a more informal setting. If he or she seems to understand, then the issue should be set aside. Remember, mutual courtesy and respect are always encouraged.

If the behavior continues, the only recourse is for a group conscience decision.*

Disruptive behavior that continues after correction makes it impossible for groups to **function** effectively. This issue may be addressed during regular group meetings or at a special group conscience meeting. We make a point of discussing the problem within the context of a meeting out of a sense of charity. We should try not to make the person who has demonstrated these behaviors feel as if he or she is being gossiped about or judged.

Repeated behavior problems that occur after this process are a different matter. The disruptive member can then be asked to stop attending meetings, until there is a demonstrated willingness to change for the good of the group.

The integrity of the group is essential to the EA program. No individual can be permitted to disrupt the group to the point where other members are made uncomfortable or decide to leave. Some groups even develop and distribute their own guidelines to highlight the importance of this matter.

Consistent issues with behavior, or even with challenges such as weekly low group attendance, low energy during

---

Maintaining Group Serenity, p. 3.

meetings, or difficulty finding volunteers to help with the meeting, can seriously affect the function of the group. These issues may indicate a need for additional soul-searching. Part of the answer may be to take your own *Group Inventory*. This piece of literature is available through the Service Center, and is similar to an individual's fourth-step inventory. It will help you diagnose and solve problems within your group.

Some problems may arise when newcomers do not feel as welcome as they might, or perhaps they leave the meeting baffled about the nature of the program. Groups that face this issue may choose to set aside a few minutes of sharing time, so that each member can both mention what brought them into the program, and welcome the newcomer. A copy of the *Newcomer Guide* may be handed out or put in your Welcome Packet—a newcomer take-home packet that outlines the program, and could include a meeting list, telephone number list (if your group keeps one), and a copy of the Yellow Pamphlet. Groups may also designate someone to meet with the newcomer after the meeting.

Some groups put a lot of effort into making their meetings work. They send out weekly meeting notices to local newspapers, have signs and greeters to welcome new members, and may even have developed good group conscience guidelines. Yet they may still find their group numbers dwindling.

When this happens, talk to your members and ask for their feedback. Broadcast a message on the EA Loop calling for ideas to keep the group running. And if these suggestions don't help, keep in mind that the Service Center may be able to help you troubleshoot; feel free to contact them with your questions and concerns.

It is very important to keep in mind that, throughout this process, we are all struggling to deal with the emotional baggage we carry each day. We must try to be as gentle and compassionate as we can with ourselves and with fellow EA members. Our goal is to create and maintain the group in a way that provides the most help to the most members.

Remember that facing sticky situations like these are difficult even in our daily lives. That makes them particularly challenging in our EA groups. There is no one best way to handle these issues. We shouldn't be critical of ourselves if we fail to correct a behavior problem quickly, or at all.

However, the reward for working hard to keep our groups functioning is substantial. We will see an increase in group serenity; the program may become more real to our members; and we'll begin pulling together to create the kind of group we'd like to belong to and grow with for a long, long time.

Help me to absorb the sunshine of the fellowship.

-Today, December 12

Sponsorship

We know in our hearts that "we can't keep it until we give it away"—that's what sponsorship in EA is all about. A sponsor is someone we can confide in without being judged. Often, having a sponsor can make the difference between just floating along in EA and making serious progress in the program.

If we've had some experience in EA and have considered becoming a sponsor, we know how difficult it can be to push ourselves to this next level of responsibility in the program.

Perhaps we've become comfortable with our recovery and are coasting along, or maybe we truly feel we are less than worthy to carry the message of EA to others suffering from emotional problems. All of us have felt these emotions at one time or another.

Sponsorship is strongly recommended in the EA program. According to the EA *Sponsorship* brochure, "Most members find it helpful to have an experienced program person with whom they build a relationship, and with whom they feel comfortable in confiding and seeking guidance in working their program." Yet an ongoing lack of willing sponsors has characterized the EA program for years. Some common misconceptions about sponsorship may be partly to blame, including:

* A sponsor must be an expert on EA, and must have worked all the steps.
* Sponsorship is a permanent relationship.
* Asking for, or offering to be, a sponsor is a sign that we are very needy.
* I'll feel rejected if my request for a sponsor is refused.
* Having a sponsor (and being a sponsor) is time-consuming and difficult.

The facts are these:
* It is recommended that sponsors have completed the fourth and fifth step of the EA program, but they do not have to have completed all 12 Steps.
* Sponsors should be somewhat knowledgeable about the program, but they are not experts.
* If we are diligent about working our steps, we may find that we feel ready to sponsor after less than a year in the program.
* Sponsorship can be ended at any time by either party. Many sponsorships develop into long-term friendships;

some sponsoring relationships do not work out. Both the sponsor and the sponsee can honestly and gently discuss the relationship and choose to end it. Keep in mind that we are working toward peace of mind and serenity in the EA program. Relationships that cause undue stress must be challenged.

* Asking for a sponsor is a sign that we are willing and ready to move forward in our twelve-step work, not a sign of weakness. Likewise, offering to be a sponsor simply tells others that we are prepared to share our recovery. It takes some faith and courage to request a sponsor and to decide to be a sponsor.

* EA suggests that men sponsor men, and women sponsor women.

* It can feel like rejection to have our request for a sponsor refused, but it is not. It is just a message that we will have to take a bit more time to find someone who is right for us. Sometimes sponsors are so busy with their daily lives (and with other people they may sponsor) that they run out of time.

* Sponsorship can be as big a task, or as small a task, as you want it to be. Often, sponsors ask that their new sponsees call or email them daily to do a "feelings and program check." Communication may decrease as the

sponsor begins to guide the sponsoree through the steps. Even hearing your sponsee's fifth step can be broken down into two short sessions to minimize time commitments.

You may be wondering what there is to gain from having a sponsor, and, later in the program, from offering to be a sponsor. Members tell us that sponsorship is often one of the most powerful elements of the EA program. Working directly with another person who's monitoring your progress vastly increases your commitment to the program. You may find that you begin to understand parts of the steps that confused you in the past. You will probably develop new confidence in your ability to work the program. You have someone to turn to on your bad days, and to share joy with on your good days. In fact, many of the Twelve Promises begin to come true more quickly for those of us in sponsorship relationships than for those who are not.

Becoming a sponsor is also a new level of commitment to the program. We are freely taking on extra responsibility, but the payoff is that our own program begins to expand and deepen. If we say a short prayer before we sponsor, we find that our Higher Power gives us the right words to say; we don't have to worry about coming up with our own words of wisdom!

Of course the best way to learn anything is to teach it. As we help other members learn the program, we find that our own comprehension of the steps and our outlook on life begins to improve.

We are motivated to work the program more consistently in every aspect of our lives—our relationships, our work, and our leisure time. The program comes to live in our hearts, rather than just in our heads. This is probably the greatest gift of all!

Let me always remember that I am growing and maturing each day, in every way, toward the good which is in me.

-Today, November 6

Optional: Charting Your Progress

Yes, of course we know when we're on track with the steps. EA is a way of life, after all. Though we may not *always* live according to its principles, we do try to apply them to most parts of our lives.

And yet . . . sometimes it may be helpful to look at a piece of paper that shows, in black and white, that our lives are gradually improving thanks to working the program.

Perhaps this closer look—a spot-check charting our progress—will reveal that we need to pay a bit more attention to Step One, Step Ten, or the *Just for Today*s. Maybe we'll decide we need to seek out a sponsor to kick-start our program, or that we should attend more meetings to alleviate our feelings of loneliness or isolation.

One EA member decided to create just such a spot-check system, using the Twelve Promises as his yardstick. This system gives you a snapshot of how well you were functioning before the program (with the promises as your guide) and how well you're doing today.

Before we begin, let's listen to the member who came up with this idea:

> I have found it useful to try to measure my progress within the program. I devised a system that has worked for me and for a few others who volunteered to test it. We tested this as we were studying Steps 10 and 11. For us, the formula definitely worked. Perhaps other EA members would enjoy working with these tools.
>
> *-Roger*

To give Roger's evaluation method a try, you'll use Chart A on page 180 ("Marking Progress Not Perfection") to rate yourself according to your achievements for each promise. Do you remember how well you were coping with life before you joined EA? Using a scale of one to 10, write down a number in the "Rating Before Program" column. Ten is the best, most capable rating, one is a low rating, and five is an "okay" rating.

Now move to the "Today's Rating" column. If you feel you're better at realizing this promise today than you were before the program, use the one to 10 scale to give yourself a high rating. If you feel you haven't made much progress, your number would be low. It's best to date your ratings, if possible, since they may change as you spend more time in the program. Also, you may rate your progress differently from day to day.

To see how far you've come, subtract your "Rating Before Program" from "Today's Rating," and place this figure in the "Amount of Change" column. Remember that both positive and negative numbers are possible. If your "Amount of Change" is positive, it means you've made headway. If it's negative, you've lost ground in working toward this particular promise.

Keep in mind that this chart reflects your achievements over **a single day.** Don't be discouraged if you've got some negative numbers on any given day. As EA members, our goal is to live one day at a time and to allow ourselves to make mistakes; we are working toward progress, not perfection.

Negative numbers may also indicate that you are facing unusually difficult challenges in your life. You may be experiencing changes in your physical or mental health, economic hardship, troubles with family and friends, job loss, or divorce. All these would significantly affect your ability to achieve the promises.

Chart B on page 181 ("Watching My Healing Grow") can be used to create a visual measure of your progress. Simply total the amount of change and divide it by 12. Fill in the date and darken the square that corresponds to your score. Soon you have a graph so you can track your own ups and downs.

Roger's evaluation charts may also be used to mark your progress in working on the *Just for Today*s. Simply jot down each *Just for Today*, rank your accomplishments in this area of life before you came into the program, and then place a figure on how well you've worked that *Just for Today* during the last 24-hour period.

The reason this system works for the 12 Promises and the *Just for Today*s is that in each case, we are evaluating specific behaviors and actions. We can easily ask ourselves how much time we spent dwelling on the past (or ignoring the past) before we came into the program. We can usually estimate how much serenity was in our lives prior to EA and examine how well our relationships have worked before and after joining the program.

Perhaps before we joined EA we had no idea how to fight the fear in our lives (*Just for today, I shall be unafraid*), had no sense of security (*We acquire a feeling of security within ourselves*), and were too wrapped up in our own problems to think about doing others a good turn. On the other hand, maybe we were skilled in some areas (*I will save myself from two pests, hurry and indecision*), but not in others (*I will take care of my physical health*).

In any case, Roger's spot-check method is simply another tool that helps us to see how our lives have changed, and what areas still need work. Feel free to use it or not—or to hold onto it for use sometime in the future. The choice is yours.

Chart A - Marking Progress Not Perfection
Rate each Promise on a scale of 1 - 10

Promises on page 237	Today's Rating	—	Rating Before Program	=	Amount of Change	Notes
Promise 1						
Promise 2						
Promise 3						
Promise 4						
Promise 5						
Promise 6						
Promise 7						
Promise 8						
Promise 9						
Promise 10						
Promise 11						
Promise 12						

Chart B - Watching My Healing Grow

Track your progress by totaling the amount of change in Chart A and dividing it by 12.
Fill in the date and darken the square that corresponds to your score. Remember Progress—Not Perfection

Score	Date	Date	Date	Date	Date	Date	Date	Date	Date	Date	Date
10											
9											
8											
7											
6											
5											
4											
3											
2											
1											
0 or less											

Part VI

Students of the Twelve Steps

PART VI—STUDENTS OF THE TWELVE STEPS

*Grant me the spirit of an eagle so I can continue
to soar and become the person You created me to be.*

-Today, December 18

Perceptions of Those Studying the Steps

Today and every day, thousands of students around the world are sitting down in their classrooms or logging on to their computers to learn about the Twelve Steps. They are studying to be psychologists, psychiatrists, drug and alcohol counselors, social workers, community health aides, and the like. This may be their first exposure to the steps. They may find the steps challenging or confusing at first. As their classes progress and they begin to draft term papers on this subject, many of them develop interesting insights.

What do they have to tell us? Most students say the steps have given them a glimpse at how human beings really work. The steps peel off the mask we put on every day and touch the inner core of our being. Some students also mention this common theme throughout the steps: revealing our weaknesses is the first step toward overcoming them.

Here are some thoughts and ideas gleaned from some student papers:

Step One—When you're drowning, you call for help. The premise of this step, say students, is simply admitting that our own coping skills have failed, and we're ready to reach out for assistance. The first step is the hardest blow to our egos, and yet it is also a step of hope. We begin to see that our mental, emotional, or addiction problems are greater than we are, and perhaps they aren't a consequence of being weak-willed or lazy.

Mouthing the word "powerless" is not enough. We must believe, deep in our hearts, that this is the end of the road for our poor behavior, emotional outbursts, drinking, or drugging. We recognize our own human limitations and gather our strength to begin taking steps toward health.

The humble acceptance of our own powerlessness paradoxically frees us to begin to accept the help we so desperately need. We will look to the group, other human beings, and our Higher Power for this help.

Step Two—Most students at least make mention of a sometimes-vexing problem: choosing our own Higher

Power. For those who still feel connected to organized religion, this can be a relatively simple step. But those of us who've been alienated by the traditional approach to religion and spirituality must now reexamine this issue.

New EA members sometimes use the group, the EA program, or nature as their Higher Power. Perhaps our own idea of whomever or whatever created the universe will serve as our Higher Power. As we consider this, many of us begin to realize that we haven't paid enough attention to our spiritual nature and we begin to put some energy into this quest. We see that faith is a leap into the unknown, a gift to be used wisely.

Once we've identified our Higher Power, we begin to marshal our resources. We see that guidance in the program will come to us in many forms: fellowship, service, reading, sharing at meetings, or choosing a sponsor. We accept that our lack of sane thinking and common sense is simply a problem that requires a solution. Our own hard work and the help of our Higher Power can indeed restore us to mental and emotional health. We can achieve our goals after all. This is not the end of the line for us.

Step Three—We make dozens of decisions every day. This step calls on us to add yet another decision to our daily list: deciding to turn our will over to our Higher Power's care. Many students use the word *surrender* when discussing this step; some even quote the adage, *Surrender equals serenity*. We are passing the baton to someone whom we believe can carry on the race.

This means also surrendering our own addictions, dependencies, and character flaws, which may have defined us over the years. Who are we without them? It can be a scary question. We realize that we are called on to trust our Higher Power to such an extent that we can embark on a long journey without really knowing when or how we'll reach our destination.

However, this step also offers us a good measure of comfort. We are invited to rest our cares and worries for a moment with a power greater than ourselves. That brings with it a deep knowledge that all will be well.

Step Four—The "thinking" steps are over now. This step signals that we are entering a phase of action—sometimes very difficult and painful—but action that is necessary if we are to recover. Our instincts may be to deny and hide our flaws and resentments, yet this step is bent on exposing them to ourselves, to our Higher Power, and eventually to another person. We realize that we must learn to love and accept ourselves just as we are in order to risk so much.

Students emphasize that we are required to meet a very high standard here, that of complete moral honesty. How many of us have set too high a standard for ourselves, only to fall short and damage our self-esteem? But that was before we joined a 12-step program.

The program spreads out a safety net underneath us. That safety net is the first three steps, which begin to break down our feelings of loneliness, isolation, and self-pity. We return to these steps again and again, until our confidence becomes strong enough to allow us to bring our own internal demons out into the light of day.

Step Five—This step begins our process of trusting another human being. The Emotions Anonymous program asks us to develop *our kinship with God and man,* a challenging process that calls on all our reserves of faith, courage, and hope.

We learn in this step that all people are not judgmental. We may have lived troubled lives with our family of chance, but our 12-step friends can become our family of choice. Closeness, community, and care for ourselves and others can replace that non-stop, negative movie reel playing in our heads. Our fifth-step person relieves our guilt feelings by listening in a loving way, allowing us to move forward from our old resentments, behaviors, and fears into a healthier future.

Step Six—After reviewing our fifth-step inventory, many of us are more than ready to have our character defects removed. This midpoint of the program is a place where we can rest and take stock of how far we've come. We see how our defects of character have shaped our lives and we appreciate how hard we've worked to reveal our problem behaviors.

We've struggled with admissions of powerlessness and have worked to develop our willingness, spiritual nature, decision-making abilities, and trust. We are ready to be changed. Still, some fears remain. We know where we've been, but where are we going? If we put our lives and character defects in God's hands, will we really become the kind of person we want to be? And how difficult will it be to teach the "old me" new tricks?

This step presents an ideal of perfection that we, as humans, will never fully attain. But just because we will never be perfect does not mean we can give up. Our lives are a work in progress; I can be a better person if I allow myself to think I can. I have become *entirely ready* when I've decided that my pain is greater than my fear and then I move on to Step Seven.

Step Seven—It's time to make our first direct request of our Higher Power, say students. We do so humbly, finally admitting to ourselves that our will has failed, and a greater will must preside.

How do we show that we have asked for help? Through patience and persistence and by listening carefully for signs of change.

We mustn't fall into the trap of thinking that our shortcomings will be removed our way and on our schedule. We realize that we must do the legwork here, but we cannot control where our efforts will lead. No magic wand will wave over us and turn our character defects to dust. We all grow slowly, gradually, and over a period of years. We can be impatient and demand results, but that will not aid us in our journey to become the kind of person we're meant to be.

Step Eight—Step Seven has given us a feeling of starting our lives anew, with a fresh slate. The people we have hurt, however, may still be suffering the effects of our past poor behavior. We must take pencil to paper once again, perhaps calling on our fifth-step material for inspiration, and make a list of everyone we have harmed. Perhaps the primary name on the list will be our own.

Not only do we develop our list, but we also become willing to make a sincere apology, and to change our behaviors to reflect our change of heart. How do we become willing to make amends to ourselves and others? The program has shown us that willingness is a function of trust and hope. We must begin to trust ourselves and learn to nurture our own spirits, with the help of our Higher Power.

We sustain hope for the future by envisioning ourselves reaching out with love and comfort to ourselves, and to all who have suffered.

Step Nine—The program now requires us to take direct action, wisely and courageously. We are called on to make good judgments about when amends may (or may not) be appropriate. Yet this is a step that moves us away from our own introspection, our own spiritual contemplation, and into a world where there are many more variables.

Often we begin to seriously contemplate this step at the same time that others are noticing how much we've changed by working the EA program.

How will our amends be received? We can often anticipate how *we* will respond in given situations because we know ourselves too well. *Others*, however, are a challenge. We may offer amends that are gratefully accepted—or our amends may be met with confusion, anger, or even outright rejection.

We will be helped a great deal by having a sponsor or other EA friend at our side, since amends-making can be an emotionally draining experience. We will want to confide in someone who can provide balance, perspective, and unconditional acceptance of our efforts. And, as always, only the efforts are ours. The results belong to our Higher Power.

Progress on our ninth step yields many benefits. We may think we don't know what to say, but somehow the right words just come to us. We become more confident of ourselves and more patient with others. Our trust in our Higher Power deepens and decision-making becomes less difficult for us. We realize that the damage to our own ego is more than made up for by our growing maturity in the EA program.

Step Ten—Having "survived" Step Nine, we are determined to quickly pursue the amends-making process in the future. We commit to a daily personal inventory that allows us to spot our errors in judgment quickly.

Sometimes this can simply be a gratitude list, reminding us of all the good things in our lives. Other times, we'll find our conscience troubles us over a particular issue or behavior until we are able to apologize to the person we have harmed.

Perhaps we still turn our anger inward and become our own worst enemy. In that case, students point out, our daily inventory is a barometer of our mental and emotional health that can help us change our behavior.

If we find we are having a series of very challenging days or weeks, we may need to contact our sponsor, attend an extra meeting or spend some time with EA literature. It's important that we try to focus on how far we've come in the program, rather than berating ourselves for our failings.

This is a lifetime program, not a quick fix. We will see ourselves growing very gradually in patience, humility, self-love, and serenity. We will stumble often, but that does not mean we aren't making progress.

Step Eleven—This step looks simple, but it can be extremely tough for those who aren't in the habit of prayer or meditation. Here we must develop our listening skills. We become able to discern our Higher Power's will for us *before* we blunder into the old self-destructive behaviors that caused us so much pain.

In a busy world, it can be difficult to allow ourselves to remain still. Our tendency is to fill our days with the pursuits of work, rest, and pleasure. But we find that if we can carve out only 10 or 15 minutes a day for reflection and communion with our Higher Power, no matter how plain our words or how divided our attention, we begin to feel better about ourselves. Our relationships with other people will improve, and we'll intuitively know how to handle situations which used to baffle us.

Step Twelve—A spiritual awakening can be compared to the opening of a bud in springtime. We hardly notice it's there. Then one day we realize that a flower has appeared where there was once only dry, bare earth. The flower, like this final step, makes its presence felt as a sign of hope and inspiration.

We, too, may be on the verge of budding. We are preparing ourselves to share our own faith, hope, love, and recovery with others. Our recovery has progressed to the point where the pain of our past is no longer our continual concern. Reaching out to others who are hurting, students say, takes the place of dwelling on yesterday.

We may find that we've acquired a feeling of security within ourselves, for ourselves, and that God is doing for us what we could not do ourselves. Certainly, it's not our own power that gets us up and talking about the program. Our Higher Power motivates our actions, directing us to meet with newcomers, offer service to EA International, assist at meetings, or even to start our own EA meeting.

The idea of carrying the EA message and practicing the principles of the program in all our affairs seems like a natural extension of our belief in the power of the steps. Although we don't preach the program, we do embody it in our thoughts and actions. We allow others to see that help and health are here. We "learned and earned" the steps, and others can, too.

We have a great deal to learn simply by listening to students of the steps. They are approaching these concepts with a fresh perspective and they can help us energize our own twelve-step program. We are grateful for their interest in the steps, enlightened by the insights they have shared, and inspired to move forward down the trail blazed by the EA program.

> *Open my eyes to see friends who can help me,*
> *and friends I can help.*

-Today, February 11

Self-Help Groups—New Thoughts and Research

We have seen a proliferation of support groups of all sorts over the past decade. Now, one can choose from more than 200 Anonymous groups, from Overeaters Anonymous to Sex Addicts Anonymous, as well as hundreds of privately run groups for physical health problems, mental health issues, and addictions.

There are grief and divorce support groups, groups for new mothers, adoptive parents, and the elderly, just to name a few. The number of religion-based support groups is also growing. The reasons for all of this diversity include a new acceptance for people admitting and dealing with their problems, rather than being stigmatized. There is also a body of research that's beginning to show that support groups really do work.

The members of Emotions Anonymous represent a broad spectrum of society. Some of our members do suffer from physical and mental health challenges. Many have substance abuse issues themselves or come from alcohol/drug-addicted families. Abuse, loss, grief, eating disorders, and divorce are all issues dealt with by our members, and many attend multiple types of support groups.

But, unlike many other groups, you needn't "qualify" for EA by having a specific disorder. In fact, delving into our various diagnoses is discouraged in EA—we usually do not place labels on any degree of illness or health.

However, a 1999 definition of the concept of mental health developed by the U.S. Surgeon General may be helpful in thinking about the general kind of support EA offers its members. *Mental health is the successful performance of mental function, resulting in productive activities, fulfilling relationships with other people, and the ability to adapt to change and to cope with adversity; from early childhood until late in life, mental health is the springboard of thinking and communications skills, learning, emotional growth, resilience and self-esteem.**

Using this broad definition, it would seem that almost all of us face mental health challenges at some point in our lives. Likewise, many of us have experienced fairly good levels of personal mental health at other points.

Now let's take a look at why self-help/support groups work. The National Mental Health Consumer's Self-Help Clearinghouse says that groups like these help members in a number of ways, including:

* Lessening feelings of isolation
* Increasing practical knowledge
* Sustaining coping efforts
* Replacing self-defeating thoughts and actions with wellness-promoting activities
* Contributing greatly to empowerment
* Offering realistic hope for the future
* Improving self-esteem
* Decreasing hospitalizations

Certainly, Emotions Anonymous can claim to have similar positive effects on its members. Here are a few examples:

Lessening feelings of isolation
EA members often form a bond or connection which goes

**Mental Health: A Report of the Surgeon General*

beyond a traditional friendship. They are a community of loving, accepting individuals willing to share their deepest thoughts and fears. Members are encouraged to attend meetings regularly, find a sponsor for increased program contact, and use the telephone list (if available) to contact other members between meetings.

Increasing practical knowledge

As members share their own experiences of working the program to gradually increase their serenity, newcomers are often inspired to try similar techniques. The steps themselves teach the skills of acceptance, self-appraisal, honesty, optimism, admitting, and righting wrongs, as well as prayer/meditation/reflection, service to other members, and being a responsible member of the community.

Sustaining coping efforts

Everyone stumbles from time to time, but in EA you are not alone with your challenges. Not only do you have the support of other members, but you have the tools and techniques offered by the program, from the *Just for Today*s to the *Slogans We Use*. There is always somewhere to turn when you feel as if your own coping efforts aren't working. Our network of meetings around the world provides a safety net, even for those who travel frequently. You are never a stranger at EA.

Replacing self-defeating thoughts and actions with wellness-promoting activities

One of EA's specialties is helping us replace "stinking thinking" with positive thoughts and actions. EA teaches us that our minds, bodies, and spirits are entwined; taking care of one means taking care of the others.

We find that paying attention to our physical health is just as important as working on our mental health and our spirituality. The process of asking our Higher Power to remove our shortcomings (Step 7) is a tangible way to work on replacing self-defeating behaviors with character assets.

Contributing greatly to empowerment

EA is a program that you do for yourself, by yourself. You have at hand all the tools you need to help you, but it is your job to make those tools work for you. Because your success depends on your own willingness to work the program, you begin to realize that you alone can change your life.

You can decide to turn your will over to the care of your Higher Power and make progress toward emotional health. You begin to take responsibility for your actions and increase your feelings of self-worth. Strangely enough, by turning over your will, you become empowered to take the actions necessary to live a happier, healthier life.

Offering realistic hope for the future

Emotions Anonymous is a program of hope. It tells us that no matter how far down the scale we have gone, we can help ourselves and others find a measure of serenity.

The program does not make promises for an unrealistically happy, trouble-free life, but it does hold out some promises for the future. The 12 Promises come true for many of us as we make progress in the program. The first three promises alone tell us we can realize a new freedom and happiness; avoid regretting the past or wishing to shut the door on it; and begin to comprehend the word "serenity," and know peace of mind.

Improving self-esteem

Many of us have been told throughout our lives that we are not good enough: not pretty enough, not smart enough, not hard-working enough. Soon this becomes the script that we use when we talk to ourselves. We reinforce this negative image and begin to feel worthless.

Now we have a way to fight back, because as we say in EA, "Our Higher Power doesn't make junk." You are a beloved human being just as you are. You can change the way you talk to yourself and feel about yourself if you choose, and you can let your unique personality shine through. Self-esteem is truly an inside job!

Decreasing hospitalizations

Stories in the EA book, as well as notes sent in by EA members around the world, tell us again and again about members finding a new level of wellness through Emotions Anonymous.

Many find they are able to decrease their medication dosages (under doctor's supervision, of course) and avoid the lengthy hospital stays that were characteristic of their past. People helping people is the secret. The support of others like you working the program to the best of their ability has a kind of healing power not found in most hospitals.

We begin to feel that there is hope. Even on our darkest days, we are accepted for who we are, and for the richness that we alone can bring to this life.

Part VII

Carrying
the Message

PART VII—CARRYING THE MESSAGE

May I remember that when You guide my life,
it goes smoother than when I try to control it myself.

-Today, May 12

Finding a Home Group

Remember when you started your first job or bought your first home? You were nervous, yet certain that this was the right step for you. Probably you looked at many different jobs or homes before settling on the right one. Choosing your home group (the EA group you attend most regularly and feel most comfortable with) is much like that process.

It may be that you chose your home group out of necessity; perhaps there is only one group within 20 miles of you. But often we do have a choice. We find that a certain night works best for us and set out to find the EA groups in our area that meet on that evening. We may find that we're comfortable at the first group we attend, but here are some additional points to consider:

* Is the location safe, particularly for evening meetings?
* Can I commit to attending on this day and time with reasonable certainty every week?
* Are there enough members so that sharing won't become repetitive, but few enough that everyone gets to share?
* Does the group follow a standardized format and abide by the concepts and traditions?
* Will I be able to locate a sponsor within this group (or could someone in the group help me find a sponsor)?
* Would I feel comfortable helping set up this meeting room, helping with refreshments, or being responsible for the key to the facility once I become a member?

Once you've thought through these issues, you'll have to see how "at home" you feel in the group. You may want to attend several different groups to compare qualities before settling on a home group. It's often helpful to take down the telephone number of the group coordinator or locate it on the meeting list sheet, to call with any questions you might have.

Starting Your Own

Perhaps you've had some experience in the program and are interested in starting a new EA group. This is the most important way the program is shared with others—a special service you can offer your community.

It is also a very important way to enhance your own understanding of the steps, traditions, and concepts, and to move your program into high gear. EA has helpful, complimentary *Starting a Group* packets that can guide you through the process. Included in the packet is *Suggested Format for EA Meetings,* which walks you through the meeting step by step.

The first move toward starting a new group is locating a meeting spot. Many EA programs are housed in churches, community centers, and hospitals, to name a few. It is often helpful to consult members of an established EA group near you to assist in this process, particularly if you are new to the community. Other members may have already thought through, or even contacted these locations, and this may save you some time and effort.

The most effective way to approach the staff at a potential meeting location is by first writing a letter of explanation to the person in charge of coordinating meeting rooms. You will have to call to get a name and address for that person.

In the letter, you will outline the basic nature of EA, briefly explain your own experience with the group (particularly if you've previously established other meetings), and mention a date and time when you will call to discuss the issue. Then follow up by making that phone call. If the contact person is hard to reach, you may have to leave several phone messages before reaching him or her.

Often these decisions can be made over the telephone, but sometimes the meeting room coordinator asks to meet with you. It's understandable that in exchange for the privilege of using their meeting space, you spend a few minutes of your time answering any questions they may have.

Many meetings are held in spots that are open to the public all day and at least most of every evening. But in some cases, you may be entrusted with a key to the building. This is a serious commitment to the building management that you will keep the key safe and use it only for purposes of your EA meeting. You must always know the whereabouts of the key, and verify the trustworthiness of anyone you lend it to.

Even if you do not have a key, remember that you do have some stewardship of the building and meeting room you use. Make sure unnecessary lights are turned off, that chairs or tables are replaced as you found them, and that your meeting is not disruptive to other events going on in the building.

Some facilities limit the types of signs you can post due to concerns about damage from tape or pushpins. And keep in mind that many EA groups offer a small monthly donation to the church or other facility that hosts the meeting, as well as monthly donations to the EA International Service Center.

To that end, the next step in putting together a meeting is establishing a bank account. EA is a nonprofit organization, and you will need a letter from the Service Center verifying this status. After that, it's easy: Walk into the nearest bank and tell the teller you'd like to speak to someone about setting up a nonprofit account, which is usually free.

You'll soon receive your first checks and deposit slips. Particularly if your meeting orders and sells literature, a bank account like this is a must. It is also part of being responsible with the donations you'll receive from your members. Trusted servants, or treasurers (if your group has a volunteer for this post), must be able to account accurately for all EA money. They should do a brief financial review quarterly, during the "announcements" part of your EA meeting.

Now it's time to coordinate the materials you'll need for your new group. You may choose to pre-purchase some literature—such as extra *EA* books, *Today* books, and *EA's Twelve-Step Program* (yellow pamphlets)—using your own money, then reimbursing yourself as funds become available.

Some groups keep records of attendance, donations, and the step being worked, by using convenient forms available at the Service Center. Likewise some groups keep optional, confidential telephone lists with first names only, and evening phone numbers. These lists must be kept in a safe spot. Members sign the list only if they freely choose to do so.

Phone lists allow members to "use the telephone as their meeting place" when they need to talk. They can be used to inform core group members when a meeting is cancelled due to severe weather.

You'll have to decide whether or not to offer refreshments and how to provide them; whether or not to use nametags or name table-tents; and what sort of signage you'll need for newcomers to easily locate the meeting. Tape, markers, scissors, and spare construction paper often come in handy, too.

All these materials should be organized in a way that would allow anyone to set up and lead your meeting. Most groups consolidate their literature and materials into a small box clearly labeled with the group name, your name, and your telephone number (just in case someone needs to temporarily relocate your box).

Often the meeting room coordinator will allow you to store the box on-site, but sometimes you will have to bring these materials back and forth. Make sure you don't store valuables or money in these boxes, especially if they are kept onsite.

Once you've established a meeting location, day, and time (often determined by what nights the meeting room is available), set up your bank account, and pulled together the basic materials for your meeting, it's time to get the word out.

Contact the Service Center as soon as possible to ensure that your new group is included in updated local meeting lists. Then turn your attention to other meetings. Established EA groups in your area will be your best allies and sources of information and support when starting a new group.

You may want to call or write each local meeting coordinator, since other groups may encourage their members to attend your meeting for a few weeks to get it up and running. Likewise, established meetings will sometimes take up a special collection to donate towards those initial expenses you will incur when starting your meeting.

Don't be shy about letting the rest of the world know about your new meeting, either—after all, helping others in need is the reason you started your group. In its *Starting a Group* packet, EA has pre-written press releases that you can customize with your name and number and send out to local newspapers and magazines. Most of these publications have a community news column where meeting notices are published free of charge, although you typically have no control over when they are published.

You may want to contact mental health units, counseling centers, shelters, alcohol and drug counseling facilities, senior centers, and county social work organizations in your area. You can do this easily by sending out *Yellow Pamphlets* or *EA for the Health Professional* brochures printed with your name, telephone number and meeting information.

Here's your chance to let others in your community know that EA has arrived. Create your own fliers (or use the suggested formats from your *Starting a Group* packet) and request that they be posted in libraries, community centers, grocery stores, coffee shops, or anywhere people gather. You'll be surprised at how many telephone calls you'll receive, especially in the first few months of a new meeting.

If you work, you may want to include a reference to EA on the outgoing message of your home answering machine and ask callers to leave a message for later. It's also helpful to have a meeting co-leader, if you can find one, to share in the responsibility of receiving and returning phone calls.

Make sure you have a state, province, or area meeting list next to your telephone. Some folks may have heard about your group from a friend and are calling to see if there's an

EA meeting near them. Remember to refer callers to the Service Center if they need additional information.

Occasionally you may receive calls from people who are extremely upset, depressed, or in urgent need of intervention. You can tell these callers, "I'm not a counselor. I can't help you with your problems. I can only tell you about EA, encourage you to attend a meeting, or refer you to the Service Center for more information. I urge you to dial 911 or call a crisis center if you feel you are unsafe."

The most important thing to remember in starting a meeting is this: you don't have to do it alone and you shouldn't. Your group members should be involved from the outset in making the meeting work. Encourage them to volunteer to be treasurer, literature coordinator, or meeting public relations person. Request a show of hands for those who will take on the role of trusted servant for a month or two, and another to solicit volunteers for setting up and taking down meeting room preparations and signs.

Service to Emotions Anonymous is not only in the best interest of EA, it is in the best interest of your group members. The more others feel a part of the meeting, the more committed they will be to attending regularly and putting maximum effort into working their program.

Your job as meeting coordinator is to diminish your own importance and let the group develop its own identity. After all, the steps consistently ask us to let go of our ego-driven desires to work for the common good.

Finally, we must say a word about handling difficulties within your group and what to do if your new meeting looks as if it won't survive.

All groups should have *group conscience meetings* on a monthly or quarterly basis. These are attended by your home group members and are aimed at resolving problems within the group (see page 164). Some problems within a group may include dwindling attendance; lack of volunteer support from members; crosstalk, feedback, or dispensing advice during meetings; and lack of respect among members.

These issues are common to most, if not all, EA meetings at some point in their existence. Feel free to ask for help with these problems from established group leaders, the Service Center staff, or on the EA Loop. You can also take a *Group Inventory* and develop new guidelines for running your meeting in accordance with the Twelve Traditions and the Twelve Concepts.

EA is our shelter from the storm as we each search for

our own serenity using the Twelve Steps. It can be stressful to participate in meetings that don't abide by the concepts and traditions, just as it may be stressful sitting alone, week after week, at meetings with little or no attendance.

If your serenity is being compromised by these circumstances, you owe it to yourself to take a break from this group. Surrender meeting coordinator duties to another member or allow members to rotate these responsibilities. The more you can turn your stress, anxiety, and fears over to the care of your Higher Power, the better you will feel about yourself.

A group left to its own devices to survive will often overcome its obstacles and carry on. If it doesn't, perhaps this group wasn't meant to be at this time. Please don't allow yourself to suffer guilt or remorse about a meeting that closes; rather feel good about your efforts and the talents you've been able to share with EA and your community. One of the blessings of Emotions Anonymous is that we touch so many lives in ways that we will never know.

May I always be the best possible example to others.
May my past experiences and future goals give
them and me the willingness to work harder
to achieve and maintain emotional health.

-Today, January 15

Putting Your 12th Step into Action

For most of us, arriving at our 12th and final step is like coming home after a long journey. We feel a strong sense of accomplishment and pride. Perhaps we even feel as if it's time for a rest after the hard work of our first steps in the program.

As we shall see, though, the 12th step is anything but a step of rest. It is the step that demands the most vigorous action in the EA program and is guaranteed to push us out of our comfort zone and into the world. Here, we break down the step and examine each element:

Having had a spiritual awakening as the result of these steps—The thought of having a spiritual awakening (a deepening of our connection to ourselves, to our Higher Power, and to others) is what keeps us working the steps. It is our reward for all of our efforts. Once we begin to sense that our spirituality has grown and matured, we see that so much more is possible for us.

Our lives can have serenity in the midst of unsolved problems, we can be an oasis of calm in a hurried world, we can experience the deep satisfaction of aligning our will with the will of our Higher Power. And far from being the end, our spiritual awakening is a new beginning.

We might be looking for a thunderbolt to strike us and announce the presence of our spiritual awakening: but like most things in life, the process is usually much more subtle than that. Working the steps allows us to rise gradually, just as the sun rises each morning. We come slowly into the light of our own lives and begin to see that joy and peace are available to us once more.

A spiritual awakening can be as small as waking up with a renewed sense of hope one morning, or as great as finally finding our true calling in life. We begin to become "at ease" with our emotions.

We are content to let ourselves acknowledge and feel our full range of feelings, to let them wash over us while keeping our heads safely above the tide. We can live there in those moments of pain or pleasure, recognizing that **we** are not **our emotions,** and that no emotion lasts forever. We can stop fighting and rest into our sadness or our joy. This too shall pass.

Perhaps we became stuck on certain steps along the way and can only look longingly at the 12th step. We may have completed all the steps and not yet felt the spirituality or serenity we so desperately seek.

We can take comfort in our Higher Power during these darker times. We can't demand to have an immediate spiritual awakening—it simply happens when the time is right. But by committing our minds, hearts, and hands to the work of the steps, we create a space where serenity can thrive. All we can do now is invite it in and wait patiently.

We tried to carry this message—How do we carry the message? We do this in so many ways we may not realize it's happening. The message of the Twelve Steps is reflected in the way we carry ourselves, in our dealings with others, in a smile we share with someone who's having a bad day. We become what we believe in.

Our friends, family, and colleagues will notice this change in our behavior. They may not always like what they see, and they may ask, "What happened to that crotchety person my aunt (or mother or wife) used to be? I could always count on her to behave in the exact same way every day, and now she's different." Or they may enjoy the new you so much that they ask you to share your secret. Perhaps their interest in the Twelve Steps begins to grow.

The message of Emotions Anonymous is also carried in many more concrete ways. Key among these is a willingness to give of yourself, to volunteer at meetings or service boards, to become a sponsor, to start a new group. We begin to want to give back to the program that has already given us so much.

This urge is very similar to the feelings that motivate some people to run for public office. They know they are taking a risk, they may well lose the race, but they so want to give back to their community that their own comfort and self-interest pales in comparison.

Have you ever wondered what your life would be like if you had never found a meeting to attend, never had a sponsor, never even heard of Emotions Anonymous? It's a frightening thought for some of us. Yet without a variety of people from all backgrounds and all walks of life committing themselves to the work of the program, that is a scenario we could have faced. Our job is to ensure that no one who is sincerely interested in becoming emotionally healthy through the 12 Steps ever has to face that prospect alone.

There's an old saying that illness starts with an "I" but

wellness begins with "we." It is tempting to sink back into the seclusion of our old way of life, even after we've become 12-Step veterans. We have to resolve to avoid that path at all costs.

Step Twelve directs us to carry the message not only by example, but also by our hard work. It's an honor and a privilege to be able to share our talents with others. Let's not let this opportunity pass us by.

And to practice these principles in all our affairs—Early on in the program, we may have tried to keep our EA life separate from our "real life." This might even have worked for a while. But as we explored the steps more deeply, we found that the separation began to blur.

Suddenly, we begin to see our program working through us at home, at our jobs, and in our intimate relationships. Our dealings with people improve. We change the way we interact with our closest family members and friends; we become more honest and more accepting. We apologize for our mistakes and avoid holding grudges.

It is said that every behavior has an emotion right behind it. We've been making so much progress in learning to face, feel, and then turn over our emotions, that our behaviors have become different, too.

We find that resorting to our old coping methods of denying, putting on a false front, lying, tantruming, or obsessing are no longer satisfying. In fact, they may be starting to cause us pain.

We've come so far in our spiritual development that our "automatic responses"—those that have been programmed into us as children or that we learned to adopt as a survival mechanism—are not so automatic any more. This is when we know what it means to practice the principles of EA in all our affairs.

The principles of EA (page 33) are honesty, hope, faith, courage, integrity, willingness, humility, responsibility, justice, perseverance, spiritual awareness, and service.

We likely have the opportunity to practice several of these, particularly honesty, integrity, responsibility and perseverance, on a daily basis. They direct our steps with regard to our interactions with others. Faith, hope, courage, and humility are personal characteristics that guide and support us during times of illness, loss, confusion, and self-doubt.

The principles of willingness, justice, spiritual awareness, and service are a bit more abstract. We have learned a great deal about willingness and spiritual awareness through our work on the steps, but may find these concepts more difficult to think about in terms of direct interaction with others.

Willingness is simply being open to instruction from our

Higher Power, rather than insisting on getting our own way. If we've ever acted in a belligerent, bull-headed, or stubborn way with friends or family, we know that willfulness rarely works to anyone's benefit. What results from hardheaded behavior is often a battle of wills that causes harsh words and hurt feelings. If, instead, our hearts and minds are willing to be open to change, we'll find that others will often respond in a helpful, cooperative way as well.

Spiritual awareness can be integrated into every area of our life; we don't have to wear a white robe and look like a guru to face problems with a certain spirituality.

As the program grows in us, we'll turn our minds more and more to matters larger than our daily cares. This will give us a thoughtful awareness in our dealings with others, enhance our decision-making abilities, and lend perspective to the difficulties we face each day. If our relationship with our Higher Power is intact, how can we become upset over a late project report, a disagreement with our spouse, or a "down" day? These things are transient, but our spiritual life—our soul—is true and constant.

The principles of service and justice are at the heart of the EA program but may not spring to mind as we get out of bed each morning.

We've discussed the importance of service to EA as a crucial way to ensure that the program is there for us and for others. But we must also consider service to our beliefs, to our goals and dreams, and to everyone we come in contact with.

We offer service when we are gentle and patient with ourselves, when we show our anger appropriately, and when we practice *turning it over* instead of *controlling*.

We are also being of service to others when we are just in our dealings with them. This means we treat our family members and coworkers fairly and respectfully. We avoid judging and comparing, which may have been an automatic response for us before we found the program.

The kind of justice referred to in the principles is not the simple "an eye for an eye, a tooth for a tooth." It is actually more of an understanding of our place in the universe.

We know that human justice is not always served; we may not see the drunk driver receive the jail time he deserves or the wealthy tycoon exposed at insider trading. But our Higher Power's justice is beyond our comprehension. We know only that we must practice compassion and concern for others, no matter who they are or what they do.

The results of our efforts will be more wonderful than we can imagine: serenity and inner peace that no human being can ever take away from us. That is the message of the 12 Steps, and Emotions Anonymous.

Keep coming back, we say. It works if you work it!

Part VIII

Our Basic Tools

PART VIII—Our Basic Tools

The Twelve Steps

1. We admitted we were powerless over our emotions — that our lives had become unmanageable.

2. Came to believe that a Power greater than ourselves could restore us to sanity.

3. Made a decision to turn our will and our lives over to the care of God *as we understood Him.*

4. Made a searching and fearless moral inventory of ourselves.

5. Admitted to God, to ourselves and to another human being the exact nature of our wrongs.

6. Were entirely ready to have God remove all these defects of character.

7. Humbly asked Him to remove our shortcomings.

8. Made a list of all persons we had harmed, and became willing to make amends to them all.

9. Made direct amends to such people wherever possible, except when to do so would injure them or others.

10. Continued to take personal inventory and when we were wrong promptly admitted it.

11. Sought through prayer and meditation to improve our conscious contact with God *as we understood Him,* praying only for knowledge of His will for us and the power to carry that out.

12. Having had a spiritual awakening as the result of these steps, we tried to carry this message, and to practice these principles in all our affairs.

The Twelve Traditions

1. Our common welfare should come first; personal recovery depends on EA unity.

2. For our group purpose there is but one ultimate authority — a loving God as He may express Himself in our group conscience. Our leaders are but trusted servants; they do not govern.

3. The only requirement for EA membership is a desire to become well emotionally.

4. Each group should be autonomous except in matters affecting other groups or EA as a whole.

5. Each group has but one primary purpose—to carry its message to the person who still suffers from emotional problems.

6. An EA group ought never endorse, finance or lend the EA name to any related facility or outside enterprise, lest problems of money, property and prestige divert us from our primary purpose.

7. Every EA group ought to be fully self-supporting, declining outside contributions.

8. Emotions Anonymous should remain forever non-professional, but our service centers may employ special workers.

9. EA, as such, ought never be organized; but we may create service boards or committees directly responsible to those they serve.

10. Emotions Anonymous has no opinion on outside issues; hence, the EA name ought never be drawn into public controversy.

11. Our public relations policy is based on attraction rather than promotion; we need always maintain personal anonymity at the level of press, radio and films.

12. Anonymity is the spiritual foundation of our traditions, ever reminding us to place principles before personalities.

Helpful Concepts

1. We come to EA to learn how to live a new way of life through the twelve-step program of Emotions Anonymous which consists of Twelve Steps, Twelve Traditions, concepts, the Serenity Prayer, slogans, Just for Todays, EA literature, weekly meetings, telephone and personal contacts, and living the program one day at a time. We do not come for another person — we come to help ourselves and to share our experiences, strength, and hope with others.

2. We are experts only on our own stories, how we try to live the program, how the program works for us, and what EA has done for us. No one speaks for Emotions Anonymous as a whole.

3. We respect anonymity — no questions are asked. We aim for an atmosphere of love and acceptance. We do not care who you are or what you have done. You are welcome.

4. We do not judge; we do not criticize; we do not argue. We do not give advice regarding personal or family affairs.

5. EA is not a sounding board for continually reviewing our miseries, but a way to learn to detach ourselves from them. Part of our serenity comes from being able to live at peace with unsolved problems.

6. We never discuss religion, politics, national or international issues, or other belief systems or policies. EA has no opinion on outside issues.

7. Emotions Anonymous is a spiritual program, not a religious program. We do not advocate any particular belief system.

8. The steps suggest a belief in a Power greater than ourselves. This can be human love, a force for good, the group, nature, the universe, God, or any entity a member chooses as a personal Higher Power
.

9. We utilize the program — we do not analyze it. Understanding comes with experience. Each day we apply some part of the program to our personal lives.

10. We have not found it helpful to place labels on any degree of illness or health. We may have different symptoms, but the underlying emotions are the same or similar. We discover we are not unique in our difficulties and illnesses.

11. Each person is entitled to his or her own opinions and may express them at a meeting within the guidelines of EA. We are all equal — no one is more important than another.

12. Part of the beauty and wonder of the EA program is that at meetings we can say anything and know it *stays there.* Anything we hear at a meeting, on the telephone, or from another member is confidential and is not to be repeated to anyone — EA members, mates, families, relatives or friends.

Just for Today
The Choice Is Mine

1. *Just for Today* I will try to live through this day only, not tackling all of my problems at once. I can do something at this moment that would discourage me if I had to continue it for a lifetime.

2. *Just for Today* I will try to be happy, realizing that my happiness does not depend on what others do or say or what happens around me. Happiness is a result of being at peace with myself.

3. *Just for Today* I will try to adjust myself to what is and not force everything to adjust to my own desires. I will accept my family, my friends, my business, my circumstances as they come.

4. *Just for Today* I will take care of my physical health; I will exercise my mind; I will read something spiritual.

5. *Just for Today* I will do somebody a good turn and not get found out. If anyone knows of it, it will not count. I will do at least one thing I don't want to do, and I will perform some small act of love for my neighbor.

6. *Just for Today* I will try to go out of my way to be kind to someone I meet. I will be considerate, talk low, and look as good as I can. I will not engage in unnecessary criticism or finding fault, nor try to improve or regulate anybody except myself.

7. *Just for Today* I will have a program. I may not follow it exactly, but I will have it. I will save myself from two pests—hurry and indecision.

8. *Just for Today* I will stop saying, "If I had time." I never will *find time* for anything. If I want time, I must take it.

9. *Just for Today* I will have a quiet time of meditation wherein I shall think of my Higher Power, of myself, and of my neighbor. I shall relax and seek truth.

10. *Just for Today* I shall be unafraid. Particularly, I shall be unafraid to be happy, to enjoy what is good, what is beautiful, and what is lovely in life.

11. *Just for Today* I will not compare myself with others. I will accept myself and live to the best of my ability.

12. *Just for Today* I choose to believe that I can live this one day.

The Twelve Promises

1. We realize a new freedom and happiness.

2. We do not regret the past or wish to shut the door on it.

3. We comprehend the word *serenity*, and we know peace of mind.

4. No matter how far down the scale we have gone, we see how our experience can benefit others.

5. The feelings of uselessness and self-pity lessen.

6. We have less concern about self and gain interest in others.

7. Self-seeking slips away.

8. Our whole attitude and outlook upon life changes.

9. Our relationships with other people improve.

10. We intuitively know how to handle situations which used to baffle us.

11. We acquire a feeling of security within ourselves.

12. We realize that *God* is doing for us what we could not do ourselves.

These may seem like extravagant promises, but they are not. They are being fulfilled among us, sometimes quickly, sometimes slowly.

How to Contact Emotions Anonymous

We invite you to attend our meetings and hope you will join us. You may find a phone number for Emotions Anonymous in your local phone book, in the support group listings in newspapers, or from community referral agencies.

You may also write Emotions Anonymous, International Service Center, P.O. Box 4245, St. Paul, MN 55104, for assistance in locating the nearest EA group. The International Service Center can also be reached by phone at (651) 647-9712, fax at (651) 647-1593, or by e-mail at generalinfo@emotionsanonymous.org. Our web site located at www.emotionsanonymous.org always has current meeting information.

If there is no group in your area, our staff will be happy to send you information on starting one. They will also answer any question you may have about EA.

Emotions Anonymous has many pieces of literature to guide you in your recovery. For a listing and description of what EA has available, you may request our catalog of materials from the International Service Center.

Part IX

Bibliography, Referenced EA Literature, and Index

BIBLIOGRAPHY

Alcoholics Anonymous
Copyright 1939
Alcoholics Anonymous

A Skeptics Guide to the Twelve Steps: What to Do When You Don't Believe
By Philip Z.
Copyright 1990
A Hazelden Book

Be Your Happiest Self
By Lauren David Peden
Excerpted in *Self* Magazine, December 2002 issue
A Conde-Nast Publication

Change Your Brain, Change Your Life
By Daniel G. Amen, MD
Copyright 1998
Random House

Five Steps to Forgiveness; The Art and Science of Forgiving
By Everett Worthington, Ph.D
Copyright 2001
Crown Publishers

Meditation
By Eknath Easwaran
Nilgiri Press
Copyright 1978, 1991
The Blue Mountain Center of Meditation
Eighth Printing, January 2002

Mental Health: A Report of the Surgeon General
U.S. Department of Health and Human Services
Copyright 1999
Published by the U.S. Public Health Service, Rockville,
Maryland

Overcoming Panic Disorder, A Woman's Guide
Lorna Weinstock, MSW, and Eleanor Gilman
Copyright 1998
Contemporary Books

*The Four Agreements, A Practical Guide to Personal
Freedom*
A Toltec Wisdom Book
By Don Miguel Ruiz
Copyright 1997 by Miguel Angel Ruiz, MD
Amber-Allen Publishing

Twelve Steps and Twelve Traditions
Copyright 1952, 1953, 1981 by the AA Grapevine,
Inc., and Alcoholics Anonymous Publishing
All rights reserved
Pocket edition, first printing 1995

Referenced EA Literature

Emotions Anonymous

Today

The New Message

Form 1	*EA's Twelve-Step Program*
Form 4	*A Personal Inventory*
Form 6	*Group Inventory*
Form 7	*Suggested Meeting Format*
Form 9	*Treasurer's Weekly Record Form*
Form 13	*Guide for EA Groups*
Form 22	*News Release Information*
Form 25	*Sponsorship*
Form 40	*The Traditions*
Form 42	*Step by Step*
Form 55	*Grief*
Form 62	*Maintaining Group Serenity*
Form 63	*For the Health Care Professional*

INDEX